The Open University

M249 Practical modern statistics

CW00551154

Computer Book 4

Bayesian statistics

About this course

M249 Practical Modern Statistics uses the software packages *SPSS for Windows* (SPSS Inc.) and *WinBUGS*, and other software. This software is provided as part of the course, and its use is covered in the *Introduction to statistical modelling* and in the four computer books associated with *Books 1* to *4*. This computer book contains all the computer work associated with *Book 4*.

Cover image courtesy of NASA. This photograph, acquired by the ASTER instrument on NASA's Terra satellite, shows an aerial view of a large alluvial fan between the Kunlun and Altun mountains in China's Xinjiang province. For more information, see NASA's Earth Observatory website at http://earthobservatory.nasa.gov.

This publication forms part of an Open University course. Details of this and other Open University courses can be obtained from the Student Registration and Enquiry Service, The Open University, PO Box 197, Milton Keynes, MK7 6BJ, United Kingdom: tel. +44 (0)870 300 6090, e-mail general-enquiries@open.ac.uk

Alternatively, you may visit the Open University website at http://www.open.ac.uk where you can learn more about the wide range of courses and packs offered at all levels by The Open University.

To purchase a selection of Open University course materials, visit http://www.ouw.co.uk, or contact Open University Worldwide, Michael Young Building, Walton Hall, Milton Keynes, MK7 6AA, United Kingdom, for a brochure: tel. +44 (0)1908 858793, fax +44 (0)1908 858787, e-mail ouw-customer-services@open.ac.uk

The Open University, Walton Hall, Milton Keynes, MK7 6AA.

First published 2007.

Edited, designed and typeset by The Open University, using the Open University TeX System.

Printed and bound in the United Kingdom by The Charlesworth Group, Wakefield.

ISBN 978 0 7492 1374 9

1.1

Contents

Introduction

This computer book covers all the computer work associated with *Book 4 Bayesian statistics*. Chapters 1 to 6 use the software package *LearnBayes*. *LearnBayes* has been written to support both the understanding and the implementation of the Bayesian statistical techniques introduced in Parts I and II of *Book 4*. The remaining chapters use the software package WinBUGS. WinBUGS is used to implement the more sophisticated Bayesian statistical techniques discussed in Parts III and IV of *Book 4*.

Using this book

As you study *Book 4*, you will be directed to work through particular chapters in this computer book. You are advised not to work on the activities here until you have reached the appropriate points in *Book 4*.

The activities vary in nature and in length. Some contain instructions on how to use *LearnBayes* or WinBUGS to perform particular tasks. Others provide practice at using the software to implement Bayesian statistical analyses; you will find solutions to these at the end of the computer book.

Conventions used in this computer book

This computer book uses the same conventions as *Computer Books 1 to 3*, with the following addition. When using *LearnBayes*, scroll buttons are frequently used when changing parameter values to produce dynamic graphics. If such dynamic graphics are slow to run on your computer, you may prefer to enter just a few values for the parameter of interest instead of using the scroll buttons. So, when scroll buttons are required, a suitable set of values to enter instead is given in the margin.

Data files

All the data files for this computer book are located in the **Book 4** subfolder of the **M249 Data Files** folder.

Chapter 1
Introduction to LearnBayes

The software package *LearnBayes* has been designed to support Parts I and II of *Book 4 Bayesian statistics*. Using it should help you to develop your understanding of the main ideas involved in the Bayesian approach to statistics. It can also be used to carry out some simple Bayesian analyses.

In this chapter, you will learn the basics of how to use *LearnBayes*. Section 1.1 contains a brief exploration of the software. In Section 1.2, you will learn how to print a *LearnBayes* plot, and how to paste a *LearnBayes* plot into a word-processor document.

1.1 An exploration of LearnBayes

This section will guide you through a preliminary exploration of *LearnBayes* to enable you to get a feel for the software.

Computer Activity 1.1 Getting started

Run *LearnBayes* now: either double-click on the **LearnBayes** icon on your desktop, or click on the **Start** button, move the mouse pointer to **Programs** (or **All Programs** — this depends on the version of Windows you are using), then to **M249**, and click on **LearnBayes**.

To exit *LearnBayes* choose **Quit** from the **File** menu.

Notice that *LearnBayes* looks a little different from standard Windows applications. *LearnBayes* is organized rather like a book. The opening screen is the **Contents** page; this lists the main topics available (**Analysis for a proportion**, **Priors**, **Likelihoods** and **Conjugate analyses**), rather like the chapters of a book. There is also a tab for each of these topics at the top of the screen. The options available within each topic are also listed (rather like sections within chapters). You will use all the options within each topic as you work through Chapters 2 to 6.

Navigation of the software is performed by hyperlinks (that is, words that are underlined), just as on the Web. When you click on a link, it takes you to the relevant part of the program. The program remembers and changes the colour of the link that you clicked, so that whenever you view the contents page you can see which options you have visited. You can discard this information or 'history' by clicking on **Clear history**. (The colour of the links will be reset when the history is cleared.)

A topic or option can be accessed directly by clicking on its name in **Contents**.

◇   Click on **Analysis for a proportion** in the list of topics and options on the **Contents** page.

The right-hand panel of **Analysis for a proportion** contains a list of the options available within this topic (namely **Likelihood** and **Prior to posterior**). At any time, any of the main topics can be accessed by clicking on the relevant tab at the top of the screen.

◇   Click on the **Priors** tab.

Notice that the layout of **Priors** is similar to that for **Analysis for a proportion**: the options available within **Priors** are listed in the right-hand panel.

◇   Return to **Analysis for a proportion** by clicking on its tab.

Any option can be accessed by clicking on it, either in **Contents** or in the panel for the relevant main topic.

◇   Click on **Likelihood** within **Analysis for a proportion**.

The left-hand panel of **Likelihood** displays a plot while the right-hand panel contains three fields. Initially, the fields contain default values and the displayed plot is the likelihood for these default values. Values can be entered in fields either by typing them in directly and pressing **Enter**, or by using the scroll buttons.

◇ Type 0.3 in the **p (Proportion of successes)** field and press **Enter**. The plot of the likelihood function will change to reflect the new values in the fields. (The value in the **x (Number of successes)** field will change to 6 automatically to reflect the new value of p, the observed proportion of successes, for the value of the number of observations n, which remains fixed.)

◇ Now click once on the upper scroll button for the **x (Number of successes)** field. As you release the mouse button, the value in the input field will increase by 1. To scroll through the numbers, click on the scroll button a second time and hold the mouse button down until the value in the input field reaches 16.

Notice that the plot of the likelihood function changes as the value in the **x (Number of successes)** field changes. (The value in the **p (Proportion of successes)** field also changes to reflect the new value of x for the fixed value of n.) In fact, the plot will change dynamically when you change any of the input fields using the scroll buttons.

◇ Now move your mouse pointer onto the plot.

Notice that the pointer has changed to cross-hairs.

◇ Move the cross-hairs until they are on the peak of the plot.

Directly underneath the cross-hairs, θ: 0.8 will be displayed; 0.8 is the value of the proportion θ on the horizontal axis for that point on the plot. The cross-hairs can be useful when investigating features of the plot.

Another way to navigate through the software is to use the **Previous Option** and **Next Option** buttons at the bottom of the window. Using these buttons allows you to step through the options in order.

◇ Click on the **Next Option** button.

You are now in the option **Prior to posterior** of **Analysis for a proportion**, because **Prior to posterior** is the option listed after **Likelihood** in **Analysis for a proportion**. Notice that the general layout of **Prior to posterior** is the same as that for **Likelihood**: the left-hand panel displays a plot, while the right-hand panel contains fields which are used to define the plot. In fact, all the options have the following general format.

• The left-hand panel displays a plot.

• The right-hand panel contains fields for inputting values.

• Values can be entered in fields either by typing them in and pressing **Enter**, or by using the scroll buttons.

• When using the scroll buttons, plots change dynamically to reflect the changing values in the fields. This is a very useful feature as it allows you to explore the effects of changes in the values.

If you are unsure which option is the next one or which is the previous one, clicking on the **Current Topic** button at the bottom of the window will take you back to the contents page of the current topic.

◇ Click on the **Current Topic** button now.

You will return to the contents page for **Analysis for a proportion** as this is the current topic.

When you leave an option, any values you have entered in the fields are lost. If you return to the option later, the default values will be displayed. When using an option, you can return to the default values at any time by clicking on the **Reset Option** button.

Using **Reset Option** is useful if you wish to clear all of the values that you have entered.

Finally, the top toolbar contains a single menu: the **File** menu is used in the same way as a menu in any standard Windows application.

1.2 Printing and pasting LearnBayes plots

Computer Activity 1.2 Printing a LearnBayes plot

If you are continuing directly from Computer Activity 1.1, then the contents page for the **Analysis for a proportion** topic will be displayed. Choose the option **Prior to posterior**, and print the plot currently displayed, as follows.

◇ Choose **Print** from the **File** menu. The **Print** dialogue box will open.

◇ Click on **OK**. The plot will be printed, together with the values in the fields that defined the plot.

Computer Activity 1.3 Pasting a LearnBayes plot into a word-processor document

Pasting a *LearnBayes* plot into a word-processor document is straightforward. You need both *LearnBayes* and your word processor running. The word-processor document in which you wish to insert the plot should also be open.

The plot currently displayed in *LearnBayes* can be pasted into a word-processor document as follows.

◇ Choose **Copy** from the **File** menu.

◇ Switch to your word processor and place the cursor in the document at the point where you wish to insert the *LearnBayes* plot.

◇ Choose **Paste** from the **Edit** menu of your word processor, and the *LearnBayes* plot will be inserted into the word-processor document.

Note that only the plot, and not the associated values in the fields, will be pasted into the word-processor document.

These instructions work for Microsoft Word and many other word processors.

Alternatively, press **Ctrl+V**.

Summary of Chapter 1

In this chapter, *LearnBayes* has been introduced. You have learned how to access the main topics and the options. You have seen that the basic layout for each option is the same, with fields on the right-hand side and associated plots on the left-hand side. You have also learned how to print a *LearnBayes* plot, and how to copy a plot and paste it into a word-processor document.

Chapter 2
Bayesian analysis for a proportion

In this chapter, you will use *LearnBayes* to investigate Bayesian prior to posterior analyses for an unknown proportion. In Section 2.1, you will explore the likelihood function for a proportion and discover how the observed data affect the likelihood. In Section 2.2, you will explore how the prior and likelihood combine to produce the posterior.

2.1 Exploring the likelihood for a proportion

Computer Activity 2.1 *Likelihood for a proportion*

In Example 3.2 of *Book 4*, the parameter θ was defined to be the proportion of adults in Great Britain who trust politicians to tell the truth. The likelihood function for θ after observing $X = 11$ 'yes' replies from 50 interviewees was given in Example 3.6, and a plot of the likelihood was shown in Figure 3.4. In this activity, you will use *LearnBayes* to reproduce the plot of this likelihood function.

If you are continuing directly from Computer Activity 1.3, then click on **Previous Option**. Otherwise, choose the **Likelihood** option from the **Analysis for a proportion** topic.

Eleven successes were observed in 50 trials. Obtain the likelihood of θ given these data, as follows.

◇   Enter 50 in the **n (Number of observations)** field.

◇   Enter 11 in the **x (Number of successes)** field.

You produced a likelihood function in Computer Activity 1.1. The method is the same here.

The likelihood function will be displayed in the left-hand panel. This is reproduced in Figure 2.1.

Notice that the value in the **p (Proportion of successes)** field changes to 0.22 automatically.

Instead of entering a value in the **x (Number of successes)** field, you could have entered a value in the **p (Proportion of successes)** field.

◇   Click on **Reset Option** to return to the default values.

◇   Enter 50 in the **n (Number of observations)** field.

◇   Enter 0.22 in the **p (Proportion of successes)** field.

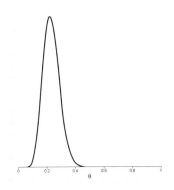

Verify that the likelihood function is the same as that shown in Figure 2.1, and that the value in the **x (Number of successes)** field changes to 11 automatically.

To allow you to explore the likelihood easily, the value in the **p (Proportion of successes)** field may be set to any value between 0 and 1, even though not all of these values are possible. When a value is entered in the **p (Proportion of successes)** field, the value for the **x (Number of successes)** field is calculated as follows: the value in the **n (Number of observations)** field is multiplied by the value in the **p (Proportion of successes)** field, and the result is rounded to the nearest integer. The plotted likelihood then uses this rounded value. See this for yourself, as follows.

Figure 2.1 Likelihood function for the proportion θ when observing 11 successes in 50 trials

For n observations, the values that the observed proportion of successes can take are $0, 1/n, 2/n, \ldots, (n-1)/n, 1$.

◇   Enter 0.23 in the **p (Proportion of successes)** field. Multiplying 0.23 by 50 gives 11.5, which is 12 when rounded to the nearest integer. Notice that the value in the **x (Number of successes)** field is indeed 12.

◇   Change the value in the **p (Proportion of successes)** field to 0.24. Check that the value in the **x (Number of successes)** field is still 12 ($= 0.24 \times 50$).

Computer Activity 2.2 *Constraints in LearnBayes*

There can be at most n successes in n trials, so x, the number of successes, must be less than or equal to n. If you enter a value in the **x (Number of successes)** field which is larger than the value in the **n (Number of observations)** field, then the value in both fields will be displayed in red to signal that the values are invalid. See this for yourself, as follows.

◇   Click on **Reset Option** to return to the default values.

The default value for **n (Number of observations)** is 20 and that for **x (Number of successes)** is 10. Suppose you wish to enter the values $n = 30$ and $x = 25$.

◇   Type 25 in the **x (Number of successes)** field and press **Enter**.

Notice that the values in the **x (Number of successes)** and the **n (Number of observations)** fields have both turned red to signal that together $x = 25$ and $n = 20$ are not valid. Notice also that the likelihood for $x = 10$ successes in $n = 20$ trials is still displayed in the left-hand panel, and the new (invalid) values in the fields have been ignored. The values in the fields will stay red until valid values are entered — that is, values such that $x \leq n$. When valid values are entered, the graph of the likelihood will be displayed in the left-hand panel. See this for yourself now.

◇   Type 30 in the **n (Number of observations)** field and press **Enter**. Since the value in the **p (Proportion of successes)** field remains fixed when the value in the **n (Number of observations)** field is changed, the value in the **x (Number of successes)** field changes to 15 automatically.

◇   Now type 25 in the **x (Number of successes)** field and press **Enter**.

The likelihood for $x = 25$ successes in $n = 30$ trials will be displayed.

There are quite a few constraints in *LearnBayes* similar to that imposed on **x (Number of successes)** and **n (Number of observations)**. In each case, the values which break the constraint will be displayed in red but the graph will not change until valid values are entered.

Computer Activity 2.3   *Effect of increasing the sample size*

In fact, in the opinion poll described in Example 3.2 of *Book 4*, 2004 (as opposed to 50) adults were asked whether they trusted politicians to tell the truth. Of these 2004 adults, 22% replied 'yes'. How does increasing the sample size n affect what the likelihood function looks like? You are asked to investigate this in this activity.

(a)   Set **n (Number of observations)** to 50 and **p (Proportion of successes)** to 0.22. Use the mouse pointer to identify the most likely value of θ. That is, identify the value of θ for which the likelihood is greatest.

(b)   Investigate the effect of increasing the sample size while keeping the proportion of successes fixed, as follows.

Use the upper scroll button for the **n (Number of observations)** field to increase the value in the field to 250. Notice that the value in **p (Proportion of successes)** remains fixed at 0.22, while the value in **x (Number of successes)** increases with **n (Number of observations)**.

Alternatively, set **n (Number of observations)** to 100, then 150, 200 and finally 250.

(i)   What happens to the likelihood as the sample size increases?

(ii)   How does the most likely value of θ, as suggested by the data, change as the sample size increases from 50 to 250?

You probably noticed that the plot of the likelihood function appears to 'jump' when using the scroll button to change the value in the **n (Number of observations)** field. This occurs because, as mentioned in Computer Activity 2.1, to enable easy exploration of the likelihood, *LearnBayes* calculates the value for the **x (Number of successes)** field by rounding the product of the values in the **n (Number of observations)** and **p (Proportion of successes)** fields to the nearest integer. For example, the value in the **x (Number of successes)** field remains at 55 for values 250, 251 and 252 in the **n (Number of observations)** field, and increases to 56 only when the value in the **n (Number of observations)** field reaches 253. It looks like the likelihood 'jumps' when the value in the **x (Number of successes)** field moves up to the next integer. (Try stepping **n (Number of observations)** through the values 250 up to 253 and see this for yourself.)

(c)   Now set **n (Number of observations)** to 2004. What does the likelihood tell you about θ after observing that 22% of the 2004 interviewees replied 'yes'?

In Computer Activity 2.3, you saw that increasing the sample size makes the likelihood narrower. You also saw that when the observed proportion of successes stays the same, the value of θ at the peak of the likelihood stays the same. Hence as the sample size increases the most likely value of θ does not change. Essentially, as the likelihood gets narrower, fewer values of θ are thought to be likely, and therefore the likelihood is more informative about θ.

Computer Activity 2.4   *Effect of changing the proportion of successes*

In this activity, you will explore how the proportion of successes observed affects the likelihood.

◇   Click on the **Reset Option** button to return to the default values: **n (Number of observations)** is 20, and **p (Proportion of successes)** is 0.5.

(a) First investigate how the likelihood function changes as p increases, as follows.

◇   Use the upper scroll button for **p (Proportion of successes)** to increase the value in the field from 0.5 to 1.

Alternatively, set **p (Proportion of successes)** to 0.75, 0.9 and 1.

(i)   How does the most likely value of θ, as suggested by the data, change as the observed proportion of successes increases to 1? (Remember that you can use your mouse pointer to identify the value of θ at the peak of the likelihood function.)

(ii) How does the shape of the likelihood change as the proportion of successes increases?

(b) Now investigate how the likelihood function changes as p decreases, as follows.

◇   Change the value in **p (Proportion of successes)** to 0.5. Use the lower scroll button for **p (Proportion of successes)** to decrease the value in the field to 0.

Alternatively, set **p (Proportion of successes)** to 0.25, 0.1 and 0.

What happens to the likelihood function as the proportion of observed successes decreases to 0?

(c) From your observations, how is the most likely value of θ, as suggested by the data, related to the observed proportion of successes?

2.2   *Exploring the posterior for a proportion*

In this section, you will use *LearnBayes* to explore the posterior for a proportion. This can be done using **Prior to posterior** from **Analysis for a proportion**.

◇   If you are continuing directly from Computer Activity 2.4, then click on **Next Option**. Otherwise, choose **Prior to posterior** from the **Analysis for a proportion** topic.

Computer Activity 2.5   *Posterior combines prior and likelihood*

In this activity, you will investigate how the posterior combines the two sources of information about θ — the prior and the likelihood.

Suppose that the random variable X is modelled by a binomial distribution $B(n,\theta)$, so that θ is the unknown proportion of 'successes'.

Suppose that you believe that the most likely value of θ is 0.25, and that θ is likely to be somewhere between 0.05 and 0.65. Use *LearnBayes* to try to match these beliefs with a prior whose mode is 0.25, and for which the probability that θ is less than 0.05 or more than 0.65 is small, as follows.

You do not need to know how *LearnBayes* does this.

◇   In the **Prior assessed values** area of the right-hand panel, set **Lower value** to 0.05, **Most likely value** to 0.25, and **Higher value** to 0.65.

Note that *LearnBayes* requires the value in the **Lower value** field to be less than or equal to the value in the **Most likely value** field, which in turn must be less than or equal to the value in the **Higher value** field. If any values are entered in these fields which break these constraints, then they will be displayed in red until they are changed so that the constraints are satisfied.

Suppose that you observe 6 'successes' in 9 trials. Enter this information in the **Observed data** area, as follows.

◇   Set **n** (**Number of observations**) to 9 and **x** (**Number of successes**) to 6. Notice that the value in the **p** (**Proportion of successes**) field changes to 0.667.

The plot of the prior, likelihood and posterior that is displayed in the left-hand panel is shown in Figure 2.2.

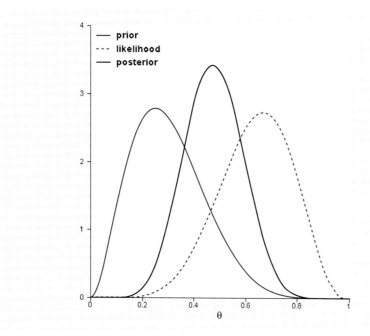

Figure 2.2   Prior, likelihood and posterior for θ

LearnBayes scales the likelihood function so that the area underneath it is 1 to make it easier to see how the prior and likelihood combine to produce the posterior. Notice that in Figure 2.2, the prior and the likelihood are similar in terms of their height and width. This means that the prior and the likelihood are more or less equally informative about θ, and as a consequence, the posterior is midway between the two.

The third area in the right-hand panel is labelled **Posterior summaries**. This contains summary measures of the location and spread of the posterior distribution. These can be used for inference to describe the posterior distribution. Notice that according to the prior, the most likely value of the proportion θ is 0.25; the most likely value of θ according to the data (as expressed by the likelihood) is 0.667; and the most likely value of θ according to the posterior is 0.472 (the mode), which is roughly midway between the other two values.

Computer Activity 2.6   Using weak priors

For the prior and data in Computer Activity 2.5, the prior and the likelihood were more or less equally informative about θ, with the result that the posterior was roughly midway between the two. In this activity, you will investigate what happens when the prior is much weaker than the likelihood.

As before, suppose that you observe 6 'successes' in 9 trials.

(a) Suppose that you believe that the most likely value of θ is 0.25, and that θ is likely to be between 0.05 and 0.9. The prior representing these opinions about θ will be weaker than the prior in Computer Activity 2.5 because the range of likely values of θ is believed to be wider. Obtain a plot of the prior, likelihood and posterior. This will be as shown in Figure 2.3.

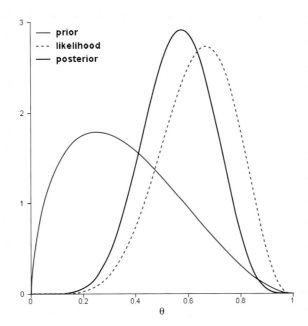

Figure 2.3   Prior, likelihood and posterior for θ

Notice that the likelihood in Figure 2.3 is exactly the same as the likelihood in Figure 2.2 because they are both the likelihood for θ after observing 6 'successes' in 9 observations. However, since the prior is wider than the likelihood in Figure 2.3, this prior is less informative than the likelihood about θ. As a consequence, the data are more informative than the prior, so the posterior is closer to the likelihood than to the prior.

(b) Now suppose that there is no prior information regarding θ so that all values between 0 and 1 are believed to be equally likely for θ. This information regarding θ can be represented by a flat prior between 0 and 1. Obtain the posterior corresponding to a flat prior, as follows.

◇   In the **Prior assessed values** area, set **Lower value** to 0 and **Higher value** to 1.

What does the posterior look like when the prior is flat? Briefly explain why this is so.

Computer Activity 2.7   *Using strong priors*

As before, suppose that you observe 6 'successes' in 9 trials. Now suppose that you believe that the most likely value of θ is 0.25, and that θ is likely to be between 0.15 and 0.35. The prior representing these opinions about θ will be stronger than any of the priors considered in Computer Activities 2.5 and 2.6 because the range of values for θ that are believed to be likely is narrower. Produce a plot of the prior, likelihood and posterior, and discuss the relative contribution of the prior and the likelihood to the posterior.

In Computer Activity 2.6, you saw that when the prior is weak and the likelihood is more informative, the posterior is more like the likelihood than the prior. On the other hand, in Computer Activity 2.7 you saw that when the prior is stronger and more informative than the likelihood, the posterior is more like the prior.

The prior opinions about θ determine the strength of the prior. What determines how informative the likelihood is? In Computer Activity 2.3, you saw that increasing the sample size makes the likelihood narrower. The narrower the likelihood is, the more informative it is about θ. Therefore increasing the sample size increases how informative the likelihood is.

Computer Activity 2.8 *Increasing the sample size*

As in Computer Activity 2.7, suppose that you observe 6 'successes' in 9 trials, and that you believe that the most likely value of θ is 0.25, and that θ will be no smaller than 0.15 and no bigger than 0.35.

Use the upper scroll button for **n** (**Number of observations**) to increase the value in the field to 100.

Alternatively, set **n** (**Number of observations**) to 20, 40, 60, 80 and 100.

(a) How does increasing n from 9 to 100 affect the posterior?

(b) Now set **n** (**Number of observations**) to 2000. How does increasing n from 100 to 2000 affect the posterior?

In Computer Activity 2.8, you saw that as the sample size increases, the posterior becomes more and more like the likelihood (suitably scaled). This is true even when a strong prior is used. Essentially this means that when you have a lot of data, the posterior will look like the likelihood, and hence will be approximately the same regardless of the prior used.

Computer Activity 2.9 *Truthful politicians?*

In Example 3.2 of *Book 4*, two priors were considered for θ, the proportion of adults in Great Britain who trust politicians to tell the truth. The first prior, which will be called Prior A, represents the belief that the most likely value of θ is 0.4, and that θ is likely to be somewhere between 0.05 and 0.9. The second prior, Prior B, represents the belief that the most likely value of θ is 0.4, and that θ is unlikely to be smaller than 0.3 or larger than 0.5.

(a) For Prior A, obtain the posterior for θ after 11 'yes' replies are observed for the first 50 interviewees, and summarize the posterior beliefs about θ. After observing that 22% of all the 2004 interviewees reply 'yes', what are the posterior beliefs about θ for Prior A?

(b) Obtain the posterior for θ after 11 'yes' replies are observed for the first 50 interviewees, using Prior B. Summarize the posterior beliefs about θ. After observing that 22% of all the 2004 interviewees reply 'yes', what are the posterior beliefs about θ for Prior B?

(c) Compare the posterior beliefs for Priors A and B.

Summary of Chapter 2

In this chapter, you have used *LearnBayes* to explore the likelihood function and the posterior for a proportion. You have seen that the peak of the likelihood always occurs when θ is the observed proportion of successes, and that as the sample size increases, the likelihood gets narrower, and therefore more informative. You have investigated how the posterior combines the information about θ contained in the prior and the likelihood. The strength of a prior relative to the informativeness of the likelihood determines the weight given to each by the posterior. You have seen that no matter how strong the prior is, the posterior will look like the likelihood if enough data are available.

Chapter 3
Exploring standard priors

In this chapter, you will use *LearnBayes* to explore normal, beta and gamma priors. There are two ways to specify a standard prior in *LearnBayes*. The first is by entering values for the parameters of the prior. Alternatively, the assessed mode and the upper and lower quartiles of the prior may be entered; in this case, *LearnBayes* will calculate the parameter values of the standard prior which gives the best match to these assessed values. In Subsection 3.1 of *Book 4*, priors were specified very informally by specifying the most likely value and a range of likely values for θ. To provide consistency with this approach, in the **Prior to posterior** option of **Analysis for a proportion**, *LearnBayes* takes the assessed values in the **Lower value** and **Higher value** fields to be assessments of the 0.01-quantile and the 0.99-quantile, respectively. (The exception to this is when **Lower value** is set to 0 and **Higher value** is set to 1, in which case *LearnBayes* simply defines a flat prior.) From now on, the more formal (and usual) method of specifying priors from assessed quartiles will be used.

The aim of this chapter is to give you a feel for each of the standard priors, and to allow you to investigate what the standard priors look like for various assessed values. You will use the options available in the **Priors** topic.

3.1 The normal prior

In this section, you will explore the normal prior.

◇   Click on the **Priors** tab, and choose **Normal** from the options listed.

Computer Activity 3.1   Specifying a normal prior using parameter values

Specify the normal prior $N(100, 50)$ using the parameter values, as follows.

◇   In the **Prior parameters** area, set **a** to 100 and **b** to 50.

A plot of $N(100, 50)$ will be displayed on the left. Notice that the values of **Mode** in the **Prior assessed value - Location** area and **Lower quartile** and **Upper quartile** in the **Prior assessed values - Spread** area have changed to match the mode and quartiles of $N(100, 50)$. Some additional numerical summaries for $N(100, 50)$ are displayed in the **Prior summaries** area.

The **Prior probability** area allows you to calculate probabilities using the prior. This can be useful for obtaining extra information about the prior for θ, and for checking that the prior is a good representation of the prior beliefs about θ. There are three fields in the **Prior probability** area: two fields labelled **c** and **d**, and a third field containing the text P(c ≤ θ ≤ d). Obtain the prior probability $P(92 \leq \theta \leq 105)$, as follows.

◇   Enter 92 in the **c** field.

Notice that the entries in the **c** and **d** fields are now displayed in red, indicating that the values in these two fields are invalid when entered together: the value in the **c** field must be less than or equal to the value in the **d** field, so that the probability $P(c \leq \theta \leq d)$ can be calculated.

◇   Now set **d** to 105.

Notice that the entries in the **c** and **d** fields are no longer red. The probability $P(92 \leq \theta \leq 105)$ is given below P(c ≤ θ ≤ d): it is 0.631. On the plot of the prior, the area under the prior between 92 and 105, which represents this probability, is shaded.

Now obtain the prior probabilities $P(\theta > 92)$ and $P(\theta < 105)$, as follows.

◇ Click on the button to the right of P(c ≤ θ ≤ d), and a drop-down menu will be displayed. There are three options: P(c ≤ θ ≤ d), P(θ > c) and P(θ < d).

◇ Choose P(θ > c) (by clicking on it). Since the value in the **c** field is 92, the probability $P(\theta > 92)$ will be given; this is 0.871. Notice that the area under the prior representing this probability is shaded on the graph.

◇ Next choose P(θ < d) from the drop-down menu. Since the value in the **d** field is 105, the probability $P(\theta < 105)$ will be calculated; this is 0.760. The area under the prior representing this probability is shaded on the graph.

The **Prior quantile** area allows you to find any quantile for the prior. This can be useful in providing further information about the prior for θ, and to check that the prior is a good representation of the prior beliefs about θ.

◇ Set the value in the **Prior quantile** field to 0.95. The 0.95-quantile of the prior is calculated; this is 111.63.

Computer Activity 3.2 *Specifying a normal prior using assessed values*

In *Book 4*, you saw that a normal prior $N(a, b)$ can be calculated to match the assessed prior value of the mode, and the assessed values L and U of the lower quartile and the upper quartile, as follows:

$$a = \text{mode}, \quad b = \left(\frac{U - L}{2 \times 0.6745} \right)^2.$$

See Subsection 6.3 of *Book 4*.

In this activity, you will use *LearnBayes* to calculate a and b for the following assessed values:

$$\text{mode} = 20, \quad L = 0, \quad U = 43.$$

Notice that the interval $(0, 43)$ is not symmetrical about the mode. However, the asymmetry is not too severe, so a normal approximation should suffice. Use *LearnBayes* to calculate the values of the parameters a and b, as follows.

◇ Click **Reset Option** to return to the default values.

◇ In the **Prior assessed value - Location** area, set **Mode** to 20.

This value will be displayed in red together with the value in the **Upper quartile** field in the **Prior assessed values - Spread** area, because the value in the **Lower quartile** field must be less than the value in the **Mode** field, which in turn must be less than the value in the **Upper quartile** field. Any values which do not satisfy these constraints will be displayed in red.

◇ In the **Prior assessed values - Spread** area, set **Lower quartile** to 0, and set **Upper quartile** to 43. Since the constraints are now satisfied, the values in the fields will no longer be displayed in red.

LearnBayes calculates the normal prior with mode equal to the assessed mode which best matches the assessed values of the quartiles. In this case, the prior is $N(20, 1016.045)$. The parameter values are displayed in the **Prior parameters** area.

The **Prior summaries**, **Prior probability** and **Prior quantile** areas all display summaries for the calculated normal prior.

◇ Calculate the lower and upper quartiles of $N(20, 1016.045)$ by entering first 0.25 and then 0.75 in the **Prior quantile** area.

The lower quartile is -1.50 and the upper quartile is 41.50. These differ slightly from the assessed quartiles because the assessed quartiles were not symmetric about the assessed mode, whereas the quartiles from the calculated normal prior are necessarily symmetric about the mode.

Computer Activity 3.3   *Exploring the normal prior*

(a) Use *LearnBayes* to calculate the normal prior which is the best match to the following prior assessed values:

mode $= 10$, $L = 8$, $U = 12$.

(b) Change the assessed value for the upper quartile to 20 and the assessed value for the lower quartile to 0. What happens to the associated normal prior?

(c) Change the assessed value for the upper quartile to 40, but leave the assessed mode and lower quartile unchanged. What is the resulting normal prior given by *LearnBayes*?

For this prior, use *LearnBayes* to calculate the probability that θ is less than 0, the assessed lower quartile. Also, calculate the probability that θ is greater than 40, the assessed upper quartile. What do you conclude about the adequacy of using the calculated normal prior to represent these assessed values?

3.2   The beta prior

In this section, you will explore the beta prior using the **Beta** option of **Priors**.

If you are continuing directly from Computer Activity 3.3, then click on **Next Option**. Otherwise, choose **Beta** from the **Priors** topic.

Computer Activity 3.4   *Specifying a beta prior using parameter values*

In this activity, you will specify the beta prior Beta$(12, 6)$ using the parameter values, as follows.

◇   In the **Prior parameters** area, set **a** to 12 and **b** to 6.

A plot of Beta$(12, 6)$ is displayed. The values of **Mode** in the **Prior assessed value - Location** area and **Lower quartile** and **Upper quartile** in the **Prior assessed values - Spread** area have changed to match the mode, the lower quartile and the upper quartile of Beta$(12, 6)$. As for the **Normal** option, the **Prior summaries** area displays some additional numerical summaries for the prior, and the **Prior probability** and **Prior quantile** areas allow you to calculate probabilities and quantiles for the prior.

There are constraints on the values of the parameters a and b of a beta prior that can be entered in *LearnBayes*. You will not be asked to enter any values that break these constraints.

Computer Activity 3.5   *Exploring the beta prior*

In *Book 4*, you saw that the values of the parameters a and b control the shape of the beta prior. In this activity, you will explore the beta prior for different values of a and b.

See Subsection 5.3 of *Book 4*.

◇   Click on **Reset Option** to return to the default values.

(a) Set the values of both **a** and **b** to 5. What are the prior mode and standard deviation of θ?

(b) Use the upper scroll button for **a** to increase the value of the parameter to 25. What happens to the shape and the mode of the prior as the value of the parameter a increases while the value of b remains fixed?

Alternatively, set **a** to 10, then to 15, 20 and 25.

(c) Now use the upper scroll button for **b** to increase the value of the parameter b to 25. What happens to the shape of the prior as the value of parameter b increases until it is the same as the value of a? What are the mode and standard deviation of Beta$(25, 25)$? Compare this prior with Beta$(5, 5)$.

Alternatively, set **b** to 10, then to 15, 20 and 25.

(d) What do you think would happen if you decreased the value of parameter a to 5? Try doing this. Were you right?

(e) Set **a** and **b** to 1. Notice that a value for the mode is no longer displayed. Why do you think this is?

The **Beta** option can also be used to calculate a beta prior which gives the best match to prior assessed values of the mode and quartiles. The method, which is similar to that used for the normal prior, is illustrated in Computer Activity 3.6.

See Computer Activity 3.2.

Computer Activity 3.6   *Specifying a beta prior using assessed values*

◇   Click **Reset Option** to return to the default values.

Suppose that you have the following assessed values:

mode $= 0.25$, $L = 0.2$, $U = 0.35$.

Use these to specify a beta prior, as follows.

◇   In the **Prior assessed value - Location** area, set **Mode** to 0.25.

◇   In the **Prior assessed values - Spread** area, set **Lower quartile** to 0.2, and set **Upper quartile** to 0.35.

Note that when specifying a beta prior, the value for **Lower quartile** must be less than the value for **Upper quartile**. Any values which do not satisfy this constraint will be displayed in red.

(a) Which beta distribution does *LearnBayes* suggest is the best match for the assessed prior mode and quartiles?

The **Prior summaries**, **Prior probability** and **Prior quantile** areas display summaries for the calculated beta prior.

(b) Is the mode of the calculated beta prior the same as the assessed prior mode?

(c) Obtain the lower and upper quartiles of the calculated beta prior. How do these compare with the assessed quartiles?

(d) Is the calculated beta prior a good representation of the prior beliefs about θ?

When calculating the beta prior from the assessed mode and quartiles, *LearnBayes* considers only beta priors whose mode is the same as the assessed mode, and from these it finds the beta prior whose quartiles are closest to the assessed quartiles. It can be difficult to find a beta prior which matches the prior assessed values exactly; often a prior which is an approximate match has to be used instead. In Computer Activity 3.6, the beta prior calculated to match the prior assessed values was a good representation of the prior beliefs about θ. However, such a good match between a beta prior and assessed values is not always possible. This is illustrated in Computer Activity 3.7.

You do not need to know how the software does this.

Computer Activity 3.7   *Matching more beta priors*

Consider the following two sets of prior assessed values.

Set 1:   mode $= 0.4$, $L = 0.3$, $U = 0.6$.

Set 2:   mode $= 0.4$, $L = 0.1$, $U = 0.45$.

(a) Use *LearnBayes* to find the beta priors which are the best matches to the two sets of prior assessed values.

(b) What is the mode for each of the beta priors?

(c) For each beta prior, find $P(\theta < L)$ and $P(\theta > U)$ for the corresponding set of assessed values.

(d) Overall, how well do the two beta priors match the two sets of assessed values?

Computer Activity 3.8   *Prior for* θ_{junk}

In *Book 4*, you assessed a mode and quartiles for θ_{junk}, the probability that you receive two or more items of junk mail each day. Find the beta prior which is the best match for your assessed values. Compare the mode and quartiles of your beta prior with your assessed values. Does your beta prior seem to be an adequate match for your assessed values?

See Activities 6.2 and 6.6 of *Book 4.*

3.3   The gamma prior

In this section, you will explore the gamma prior using the **Gamma** option of **Priors**.

If you are continuing directly from Computer Activity 3.8, then click on **Next Option**. Otherwise, choose **Gamma** from the **Priors** topic.

Computer Activity 3.9   *Specifying a gamma prior using parameter values*

Specify the gamma prior Gamma$(6, 4)$ by setting **a** to 6 and **b** to 4 in the **Prior parameters** area.

(a) What are the prior mode and mean?

(b) What is the probability that θ is less than 2?

(c) Obtain the 0.95-quantile of Gamma$(6, 4)$.

Computer Activity 3.10   *Exploring the gamma prior*

The shape of the gamma prior is determined by the values of the parameters a and b. In this activity, you will explore how changing the parameter values affects the gamma prior.

◇   Click **Reset Option** to return to the default values.

(a) Set the values for **a** and **b** to 2. Describe the shape of the prior. What are the prior mode and standard deviation of Gamma$(2, 2)$?

(b) Use the upper scroll button for **a** to increase the value of the parameter to 20. What happens to the shape of the prior, and to its mode and standard deviation, as the value of parameter a increases while the value of b remains fixed?

Alternatively, set **a** to 5, then to 10, 15 and 20.

(c) Now use the upper scroll button for **b** to increase the value of the parameter to 20. What happens to the shape of the prior as the value of b increases until it is equal to a? What are the mode and standard deviation of Gamma$(20, 20)$? How does this prior compare with the prior Gamma$(20, 2)$ that you obtained in part (b)?

Alternatively, set **b** to 5, then to 10, 15 and 20.

(d) Now decrease **a** to 2 (but leave **b** unchanged). What happens to the shape of the prior as the value of parameter a decreases? What are the mode and standard deviation of Gamma$(2, 20)$? How does this prior compare with Gamma$(2, 2)$, which you described in part (a)?

(e) Use your findings to summarize the roles of the parameters a and b.

Computer Activity 3.11   Specifying a gamma prior using assessed values

The **Gamma** option can be used to calculate the gamma prior which provides the best match to prior assessed values of the mode and quartiles. The method is the same as for beta priors.

See Computer Activity 3.6.

◇   Click **Reset Option** to return to the default values.

Suppose that you have the following assessed values:

$$\text{mode} = 2, \quad L = 1.75, \quad U = 3.2.$$

Use these values to specify a gamma prior, as follows.

◇   In the **Prior assessed value - Location** area, set **Mode** to 2.

◇   In the **Prior assessed values - Spread** area, set **Lower quartile** to 1.75. The values in the **Lower quartile** and the **Upper quartile** fields will be displayed in red because the value for **Lower quartile** must be less than the value for **Upper quartile**.

◇   In the **Prior assessed values - Spread** area, set **Upper quartile** to 3.2. The values in the fields will no longer be red.

(a) What gamma distribution does *LearnBayes* suggest is the best match for the assessed prior mode and quartiles?

The **Prior summaries**, **Prior probability** and **Prior quantile** areas display summaries for the calculated gamma prior.

(b) Is the mode of the calculated gamma prior the same as the assessed prior mode?

(c) Obtain the lower and upper quartiles of the calculated gamma prior. Compare these with the assessed quartiles.

(d) Is the calculated gamma prior a good representation of the prior beliefs about θ?

As for the beta prior, it can be difficult to find a gamma prior which matches the prior assessed values exactly, and often a prior which is an approximate match has to be used instead. *LearnBayes* identifies the gamma prior whose mode is the same as the assessed mode, and whose quartiles are closest to the assessed quartiles. Therefore it is worth comparing the quartiles of the gamma prior with the assessed quartiles to check that the gamma prior suggested by *LearnBayes* is an adequate representation of the beliefs.

You do not need to know how the software does this.

Computer Activity 3.12   Prior for θ_{phone}

In *Book 4*, the parameter θ_{phone} was defined to be the mean number of telephone calls that you receive each week. You assessed a mode and quartiles for θ_{phone} in Activities 6.2 and 6.6, respectively. Use *LearnBayes* to find the gamma prior which is the best match for your assessed values. Does your gamma prior seem to be an adequate match for your assessed values?

Summary of Chapter 3

In this chapter, you have used *LearnBayes* to explore three standard families of priors — the normal, beta and gamma families. You have investigated the shapes of these priors for various parameter values. You have also used *LearnBayes* to find the prior which is the best match for given assessed values of the prior mode and quartiles. You have seen that an exact match between a standard prior and the assessed values is not always possible. Once a prior has been found which is the best match to the assessed values, it is always worth checking how close the quartiles of the prior are to the assessed values. If the values for the calculated prior are judged to be too far from the assessed values, then it may not be possible to use a standard prior as an approximation to the opinions about the parameter.

Chapter 4
Exploring normal, binomial and Poisson likelihoods

In this chapter, you will use the options available in the **Likelihoods** topic to explore the normal, binomial and Poisson likelihoods and to investigate how the observed data affect these likelihoods.

Computer Activity 4.1   *Exploring the normal likelihood*

In this activity, you will explore the normal likelihood.

◇   Click on the **Likelihoods** tab and choose **Normal data**.

Suppose that data are observed, and that they are modelled using a normal distribution with unknown mean θ and known population variance σ^2. Obtain the normal likelihood after observing a sample of size 5 with sample mean $\bar{x} = 10$, when $\sigma^2 = 1$, as follows.

◇   In the **Data summaries** area, set **Number of observations** to 5 and **Sample mean** to 10.

◇   In the **Assumed known** area, set **Population variance** to 1.

(a)   Describe the shape of the resulting normal likelihood for θ.

(b)   Use the upper scroll button for **Sample mean** to increase the value in the field to 30. How does the normal likelihood change as the sample mean $\bar{x}$ increases?

> Alternatively, set **Sample mean** to 15, then to 20, 25 and 30.

(c)   Use the upper scroll button for **Population variance** to increase the population variance σ^2 to 20. How does the normal likelihood change as the (known) population variance increases?

> Alternatively, set **Population variance** to 5, then to 10, 15 and 20.

(d)   Use the upper scroll button for **Number of observations** to increase the sample size n to 100. How does the normal likelihood change as the sample size increases?

> Alternatively, set **Number of observations** to 25, then to 50, 75 and 100.

(e)   From your observations, how is the most likely value of θ, according to the normal likelihood, related to n, $\bar{x}$ and σ^2?

In Computer Activity 4.1, you saw that the normal likelihood is always symmetric about its peak, which occurs when $\theta = \bar{x}$. The location of the likelihood is dictated by $\bar{x}$, whereas its width is affected by both n and σ^2. The larger the sample size n is, the narrower, and therefore more informative, is the likelihood. On the other hand, the larger the population variance σ^2 is, the wider, and therefore less informative, is the likelihood.

Computer Activity 4.2   *Exploring a binomial likelihood*

In Section 2.1, you used *LearnBayes* to explore the likelihood for a proportion. In fact, you explored a binomial likelihood. In this activity, you will explore the binomial likelihood further.

If you are continuing directly from Computer Activity 4.1, then click on **Next Option**. Otherwise, choose **Binomial data** from the **Likelihoods** topic.

(a) First obtain the binomial likelihood for θ, the unknown proportion of 'successes', after observing $x = 2$ 'successes' in $n = 10$ trials, as follows.

    ◇ In the **Data summaries** area, set **n (Number of observations)** to 10 and **x (Number of successes)** to 2. The value of **p (Proportion of successes)** changes to 0.2 automatically.

    Describe the shape of this binomial likelihood.

(b) Use the upper scroll button for **p (Proportion of successes)** to increase the value of p to 0.8. What happens to the shape of the likelihood as you do this?

> Alternatively, set **p (Proportion of successes)** to 0.4, then to 0.5, 0.6 and 0.8.

(c) Use the upper scroll button for **n (Number of observations)** to increase the number of trials n to 100. How does the binomial likelihood change with increasing sample size?

> Alternatively, set **n (Number of observations)** to 20, then to 40, 60, 80 and 100.

(d) From your observations, how is the most likely value of θ, according to the likelihood, related to n, x and p?

In Computer Activity 4.2, you saw that the peak of the binomial likelihood is always at $\theta = p$, and that the shape of the likelihood depends on whether p is less than 0.5 or greater than 0.5. Also, the binomial likelihood becomes narrower as the sample size n increases.

Computer Activity 4.3   *Exploring the Poisson likelihood*

In this activity, you will explore the Poisson likelihood.

If you are continuing directly from Computer Activity 4.2, then click on **Next Option**. Otherwise, choose **Poisson data** from the **Likelihoods** topic.

(a) First obtain the Poisson likelihood for the Poisson mean θ after observing a sample of size $n = 5$ with sample mean $\bar{x} = 1$, as follows.

    ◇ In the **Data summaries** area, set **Number of observations** to 5 and **Sample mean** to 1.

    Describe the shape of this Poisson likelihood.

(b) Use the upper scroll button for **Sample mean** to increase the sample mean to 20. What happens to the shape of the Poisson likelihood as the sample mean $\bar{x}$ increases?

> Alternatively, set **Sample mean** to 2, then to 5, 10, 15 and 20.

(c) What do you think will happen to the Poisson likelihood as the sample size n increases? Use the upper scroll button for **Number of observations** to increase the value to 100, in order to see if you were right.

> Alternatively, set **Number of observations** to 25, then to 50, 75 and 100.

(d) From your observations, how is the most likely value of θ, according to the likelihood, related to n and $\bar{x}$?

In Computer Activity 4.3, you saw that the peak of the Poisson likelihood is always at $\theta = \bar{x}$. You also saw that the Poisson likelihood is right-skew for small values of $\bar{x}$, and becomes less skewed (and wider) as $\bar{x}$ increases. It becomes narrower, and therefore more informative, as the sample size n increases.

Summary of Chapter 4

In this chapter, you have explored the normal, binomial and Poisson likelihoods. You have seen that the normal likelihood is always symmetric, whereas the binomial and Poisson likelihoods are not. The peaks of the normal and Poisson likelihoods are both at $\theta = \overline{x}$; the binomial likelihood has its peak at $\theta = p$. All three likelihoods become narrower as the sample size increases.

Chapter 5
Posteriors in conjugate models

In this chapter, you will use the options available in the **Conjugate analyses** topic to obtain posteriors for the normal/normal, beta/binomial and gamma/Poisson models. For each conjugate model, the prior and data must be specified. *LearnBayes* then calculates the associated posterior, and produces a plot of the posterior, together with the prior and the likelihood. Some summary measures for the posterior are also displayed.

The method, which is essentially the same for the three conjugate models, is illustrated in Computer Activities 5.1 and 5.2 for the normal/normal model.

Computer Activity 5.1   *Obtaining the posterior in the normal/normal model*

Suppose that data are modelled by a normal distribution $N(\mu, 10)$, that the prior for μ is $N(5, 4)$ and that a sample of 15 observations has mean $\overline{x} = 1.3$.

◇   Click on the **Conjugate analyses** tab and choose **Normal/normal**.

(a)   First enter the information about the prior for μ, as follows.

◇   In the **Prior parameters** area, set the value of **a** to 5, and set the value of **b** to 4.

After the values of **a** and **b** have been set, the values for **L**, **m** and **U** in the **Prior assessed values** area change so that **L**, **m** and **U** are the lower quartile, mode and upper quartile of $N(5, 4)$, respectively. These are 3.651, 5 and 6.349, respectively.

(b)   A sample of 15 observations has mean $\overline{x} = 1.3$. The data are assumed to be adequately modelled by a normal distribution $N(\mu, 10)$. Therefore the population variance σ^2 is assumed to be 10.

Enter this information about the data, as follows.

◇   In the **Assumed known** area, set **Population variance** to 10.

◇   In the **Data summaries** area, set **n (Number of observations)** to 15 and **Sample mean** to 1.3.

A plot will be displayed showing the prior, likelihood and posterior for μ. This is shown in Figure 5.1 (overleaf).

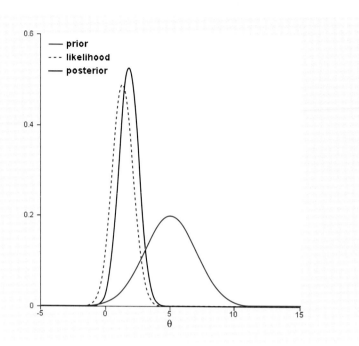

Figure 5.1 Prior, likelihood and posterior

For this prior and these data, the posterior is much closer to the likelihood than to the prior because the likelihood is stronger, and is therefore more informative about μ.

Some summaries of the posterior distribution are displayed in the **Posterior summaries** area; for example, the posterior mean and variance of μ are 1.83 and 0.57, respectively.

The areas below the **Posterior summaries** area are used for Bayesian inference; these will be discussed in Chapter 6.

Computer Activity 5.2   *Using prior assessed values*

The options of **Conjugate analyses** can be used to calculate the prior, and hence the posterior, when only the prior's assessed values of the mode and quartiles are given. This is illustrated for the normal/normal model in this activity. *LearnBayes* calculates the normal prior which best matches the prior assessed mode and quartiles, and displays the parameter values in the **Prior parameters** area.

◇   Click on **Reset Option** to return to the default values for the normal/normal model.

The value for **L** (the lower quartile) must be less than the value for **m** (the mode), which in turn must be less than the value for **U** (the upper quartile). If any values are entered that do not satisfy these constraints, they will be displayed in red.

This constraint is the same as that used when specifying the normal prior in the **Normal** option of **Priors**.

In Computer Activity 5.1, the lower quartile, the mode and the upper quartile for the normal prior $N(5, 4)$ were found to be 3.651, 5 and 6.349, respectively.

◇   In the **Prior assessed values** area, set **L** to 3.651, **m** to 5 and **U** to 6.349.

The parameters of the normal prior which provides the best match for these values will be displayed in the **Prior parameters** area. In this case, $N(5, 4)$ should fit these assessed values exactly. Verify that the values for **a** and **b** are indeed 5 and 4, respectively.

Computer Activity 5.3   *Using a uniform prior*

One aspect of the **Normal/normal** option which has not so far been mentioned is the **Uniform** button. This allows you to specify a uniform prior, rather than a normal prior, for normal data. The use of a uniform prior is illustrated in this activity.

◇   Click on the **Uniform** button.

Notice that fields for **a**, **b**, **L**, **m** and **U** for a normal prior are no longer displayed as these are no longer relevant. Notice also that the labelling on the **Uniform** button has changed to **Manual**.

In the resulting plot, the posterior and the likelihood coincide, because when using a uniform prior, the posterior is the same as the (scaled) likelihood.

◇   Click on the **Manual** button to revert to specifying values for **a**, **b**, **L**, **m** and **U**.

This prior is an improper uniform prior, as discussed in Subsection 8.4 of *Book 4*.

Using *LearnBayes* with the beta/binomial or gamma/Poisson models is the same as for the normal/normal model except that you do not need to specify a population variance. Additionally, for the beta/binomial model, instead of the sample mean, either the number of successes or the proportion of observed successes must be specified. You will use *LearnBayes* for the beta/binomial model in Computer Activities 5.4 and 5.5, and for the gamma/Poisson model in Computer Activity 5.6.

Computer Activity 5.4   *Beta / binomial model*

In this activity, you will use the **Beta/binomial** option of **Conjugate analyses** to explore the beta/binomial model.

If you are continuing directly from Computer Activity 5.3, then click on **Next Option**. Otherwise, choose **Beta/binomial** from the **Conjugate analyses** topic.

Suppose that a random variable X is modelled by a binomial distribution $B(10, \theta)$, that the beta prior Beta$(8, 15)$ is chosen for θ, and that the value of X is subsequently observed to be 7.

(a)   With this prior and these data, do you think the posterior will be closer to the prior or to the likelihood? Use *LearnBayes* to obtain a plot of the prior, likelihood and posterior. Were you right?

(b)   What do you think will happen to the prior and the posterior if you increase the value in the **m** field? Use the upper scroll button for **m** to increase the value to 0.503, while keeping the values in the **L** and **U** fields fixed. Were you right?

There are constraints on the values of the parameters a and b of a beta prior that can be entered in *LearnBayes*. You will not be asked to enter any values that break these constraints.

Alternatively, set **m** to 0.353, then to 0.403, 0.453 and finally 0.503.

Computer Activity 5.5   *Another beta / binomial model*

In this activity, you will use the same data as in Computer Activity 5.4, but a different prior.

(a)   Suppose that the prior assessed value of the mode is 0.5, and the prior assessed values of the lower and upper quartiles are 0.25 and 0.75, respectively. Obtain the plot of the prior, likelihood and posterior. Which prior has *LearnBayes* matched to the assessed values? Explain why the plot looks as it does.

(b)   Use the upper scroll button for **m** to increase the mode to 1. Now use the lower scroll button for **m** to decrease the mode to 0. What happens to the prior as you do this? Explain why this happens.

Alternatively, set **m** to 0.7, 0.9 and 1, then to 0.5, 0.3, 0.1 and finally 0.

Computer Activity 5.6   Gamma/Poisson model

In this activity, you will use the **Gamma/Poisson** option of **Conjugate analyses** to explore the posterior in the gamma/Poisson model.

If you are continuing directly from Computer Activity 5.5, then click on **Next Option**. Otherwise, choose **Gamma/Poisson** from the **Conjugate analyses** topic.

In *Book 4*, the random variable X, which represents the number of cases of foodborne botulism occurring in one year in England and Wales, was modelled by a Poisson distribution with mean μ. The number of cases occurring in each year from 1998 to 2005 was given in Table 8.1; for these data, $n = 8$ and $\overline{x} = 0.75$. A gamma prior Gamma(1.5, 0.5) was suggested.

See Example 8.3 of Book 4.

(a) Find the mode and quartiles of the prior for μ.

(b) Obtain a plot of the prior, likelihood and posterior.

(c) Use the upper scroll button to increase the value in the **m** field to 10, while keeping the values in the **L** and **U** fields fixed at their current values. Describe what happens to the prior and the posterior as you do this.

*Alternatively, set **m** to 2, then to 3, 6 and finally 10.*

Summary of Chapter 5

In this chapter, you have learned how to use *LearnBayes* to obtain posterior distributions for the normal/normal, the beta/binomial and the gamma/Poisson conjugate models. You have also used a uniform prior. You have specified a prior using either its parameter values or assessed values of the prior mode and quartiles.

Chapter 6
Bayesian inference

In this chapter, you will use the options available in **Conjugate analyses** for Bayesian inference in the normal/normal, beta/binomial and gamma/Poisson conjugate models. In Chapter 5, you used these options to obtain conjugate posteriors. You saw that once the prior and data have been specified, a plot of the prior, likelihood and posterior is produced, together with the posterior mean, median, mode, standard deviation and variance. Posterior probabilities, posterior quantiles, equal-tailed credible intervals and HPD credible intervals can also be calculated. The method is illustrated for a normal/normal model in Computer Activity 6.1.

Computer Activity 6.1   Alzheimer's progression

A normal/normal model for the natural progression of Alzheimer's disease is described in *Book 4*. The parameter of interest is θ, the mean change in the value of an index measuring various aspects of short-term memory, one year after the diagnosis of Alzheimer's disease. Changes in the index are assumed to be adequately modelled by a normal distribution $N(\theta, 100)$. A researcher suggested the normal prior $N(-25, 64)$ for θ. The progression of disease in

See Example 8.4 of Book 4.

20 newly-diagnosed Alzheimer's patients was monitored, and for these 20 patients, the sample mean of the change in the value of the index is $\bar{x} = -36$.

(a) Obtain a plot of the prior, likelihood and posterior for θ.

(b) In *Book 4*, the posterior mean and variance were calculated to be -35.2 and 4.64, respectively. Are the posterior mean and variance for θ given by *LearnBayes* the same as these values?

(c) The **Posterior probability** area can be used to calculate probabilities using the posterior. There are three fields: two fields labelled **c** and **d**, and a third field containing the text P(c ≤ θ ≤ d). Obtain the posterior probability $P(-40 \le \theta \le -35 | \text{data})$, as follows.

◇ Enter the value **-40** in the **c** field and **-35** in the **d** field. The value of the posterior probability will be given on the right-hand side of the **Posterior probability** area; it is 0.525. Notice that in the plot, the area under the posterior between -40 and -35, which represents this probability, is shaded.

Note that P(c ≤ θ ≤ d) is the first item in a drop-down menu; when it is chosen, the value in the **c** field must always be less than or equal to the value in the **d** field. When this is not the case, the values in these fields are displayed in red to indicate that together the entries are invalid.

Now obtain the posterior probability $P(\theta > -40 | \text{data})$, as follows.

◇ Choose P(θ > c) from the drop-down menu, and the value of the probability will be given; this is 0.987. The area under the posterior representing this probability will be shaded on the plot.

Now calculate the posterior probability that θ is less than -35, given these data.

(d) Posterior quantiles can be calculated using the **Posterior quantile** area. A value between 0 and 1 must be entered in the field to identify the quantile required.

Find the 0.95-quantile of the posterior.

(e) An equal-tailed credible interval is specified by entering the level required in the field in the **Posterior equal-tailed credible interval** area.

Obtain the 90% posterior equal-tailed credible interval for θ. Explain why the upper limit of this interval is equal to the 0.95-quantile of the posterior.

(f) To calculate an HPD credible interval, the required percentage level must be entered in the field in the **Posterior HPD** area. Set this value to 90 to produce a 90% HPD credible interval. Explain why the 90% HPD credible interval is the same as the 90% equal-tailed credible interval that you obtained in part (e).

(g) Summarize how the data have changed the prior beliefs about θ.

Computer Activity 6.2   *Memory tests*

In Example 5.2 of *Book 4*, the parameter θ was defined to be the mean improvement on a memory test of epilepsy patients who do not have surgery. The improvement in score from the first test to the second test for a randomly chosen patient is modelled by the normal distribution, $N(\theta, 90)$. The improvement in score was observed for 12 patients, and the sample mean $\bar{x}$ was 7.5.

(a) Obtain a plot of the prior, likelihood and posterior for θ when a uniform prior is used. Write down the posterior distribution.

(b) Calculate the posterior probability that there is an improvement on the test, that is, find $P(\theta > 0 | \text{data})$.

(c) Obtain the 99% HPD credible interval. What will the 99% posterior equal-tailed credible interval be?

In Activity 6.7 of *Book 4*, you were asked to collect junk mail and telephone call data. You will need the data in order to do Computer Activities 6.3 and 6.4. If necessary, you should postpone working through these activities until you have collected the data.

Computer Activity 6.3   Inference for θ_{junk}

The parameter θ_{junk} is defined to be the probability that you receive two or more items of junk mail in a day. In Activities 6.2 and 6.6 of *Book 4*, you assessed a mode and quartiles for θ_{junk}, and in Activity 6.7 you were asked to collect junk mail data.

In Computer Activity 3.8, you found the beta prior which is the best match for your assessed values.

(a) Use your prior assessed values for the mode and quartiles of θ_{junk}, and the data that you collected, to obtain your posterior for θ_{junk}. Is your prior or your likelihood more informative?

(b) Use your posterior to calculate the posterior probability that θ_{junk} is greater than 0.5.

(c) Calculate both the 95% equal-tailed credible interval and the 95% HPD credible interval for θ_{junk}. Why are your two intervals unlikely to be exactly the same?

Computer Activity 6.4   Inference for θ_{phone}

The parameter θ_{phone} is defined to be the mean number of telephone calls that you receive per week. In Activities 6.2 and 6.6 of *Book 4*, you assessed a mode and quartiles for θ_{phone}, and in Activity 6.7 you collected telephone call data.

In Computer Activity 3.12, you found the gamma prior which is the best match for your assessed values.

(a) Use your prior assessed values for the mode and quartiles for θ_{phone} and the data that you collected to obtain your posterior for θ_{phone}. Which is more informative, your prior or your likelihood?

(b) Use your posterior to calculate the posterior probability that θ_{phone} is less than 5.

(c) Calculate both the 95% equal-tailed credible interval and the 95% HPD interval for θ_{phone}.

Summary of Chapter 6

In this chapter, you have used *LearnBayes* for Bayesian inference in the normal/normal, beta/binomial and gamma/Poisson conjugate models. For a given prior and data, *LearnBayes* automatically produces a plot and numerical summaries of the posterior. You have learned how to obtain posterior probabilities, posterior quantiles, equal-tailed credible intervals and HPD credible intervals.

Chapter 7
Introduction to WinBUGS

WinBUGS is a software package for performing stochastic simulation for Bayesian analysis. It is non-commercial software, written and developed by academic statisticians from the MRC Biostatistics Unit in Cambridge, UK, and Imperial College, London, UK. WinBUGS is a Windows version of an earlier program called BUGS (**B**ayesian inference **U**sing **G**ibbs **S**ampling). The curiously named 'Gibbs sampling' is simply a particular method of stochastic simulation. BUGS is also the name of the high-level programming language which WinBUGS uses to define and encode Bayesian models.

In Section 7.1, the basics of WinBUGS will be introduced, including fundamentals such as starting and stopping WinBUGS. In Section 7.2, you will learn how to paste output from WinBUGS into a word-processor document, and how to print output produced in WinBUGS.

7.1 Getting started

Computer Activity 7.1 Running WinBUGS

Run WinBUGS now: double-click on the **WinBUGSxx** icon on your desktop (where xx is the version number).

The **WinBUGS Licence** window will be displayed. This contains licence and copyright information. Close the licence window.

The **WinBUGSxx** window will remain. At the top of the window is a menu bar (with menus **File**, **Tools**, **Edit**, . . .), and at the bottom of the window is a status bar, which will be empty. Between these is a blank space in which other windows will be placed.

You can view the contents of a menu listed in the menu bar by clicking on its menu name. For example, click on **File** to view the contents of the **File** menu. Some of the menus will not be used in this course.

In WinBUGS, *compound documents* are the basic medium through which WinBUGS input and output are processed, displayed and recorded. Compound documents are files with extension **.odc**. All the WinBUGS files used in this computer book are in the **Book 4** subfolder of the **M249 Data Files** folder.

Computer Activity 7.2 Opening a WinBUGS compound document

In this activity, you will open the WinBUGS compound document **dogs1.odc**.

◇   Start WinBUGS, if it is not already running.

◇   Choose **Open. . .** from the **File** menu (by clicking on it). The **Open** dialogue box will open. Notice that the **Files of type** field shows Document(*.odc).

◇   Click on the **My Documents** icon to the left of the main panel.

◇   In the main panel, double-click on the folder **M249 Data Files**.

◇   Double-click on the **Book 4** subfolder.

◇   Open the file **dogs1.odc** by double-clicking on its name.

The document will be displayed as a window named **dogs1** located in the middle area of the main **WinBUGSxx** window.

Alternatively, you can open a file by clicking on its name to select it, then on **Open**; or you can type its name in the **File Name** field, then click on **Open**.

29

Computer Activity 7.3   Closing a WinBUGS compound document

In WinBUGS, it is easy to end up with many compound documents open at the
same time, thus cluttering up the screen. In general, a WinBUGS compound
document can be closed whilst leaving WinBUGS running, as follows.

◇   Make sure the document is 'active' by clicking anywhere in the document
window. (When a window is active, the window title bar is blue, rather than
grey.)

◇   Choose **Close** from the **File** menu.

Close the **dogs1** window now.

> The concept of an active
> window is only relevant when
> more than one window is open.
>
> Alternatively, the active
> (document) window can be
> closed by clicking on the button
> marked **x** at the right-hand end
> of the document window title
> bar.

Computer Activity 7.4   Exiting WinBUGS

At any time, you can exit from WinBUGS by choosing **Exit** from the **File** menu
(by clicking on it).

Exit from WinBUGS now.

7.2   Dealing with WinBUGS output

WinBUGS compound documents provide a means for presenting all output, both
text and graphics, in a convenient form. WinBUGS has its own word-processing
facilities for editing a compound document. Altering text in compound documents
will not be assessed, but the facilities are there if you wish to use them.

The **Attributes** menu in the menu bar contains items for changing the
appearance of text in a WinBUGS document. The size, colour and font used for
the text can all be altered. There are also options for **bold**, *italic* and underlined
text.

In addition to the word-processing facilities available through the **Attributes**
menu, the **Text** menu contains some facilities for altering the appearance of text
in a compound document, but they will not be discussed in this book. However,
the **Text** menu contains a facility for finding (and/or replacing) words or strings
of characters in a compound document, which you may find useful. This facility is
obtained by choosing **Find/Replace...** from the **Text** menu.

You may prefer to use your word processor for displaying your results.
Incorporating the contents of a WinBUGS window into a word-processor
document is straightforward using standard cut-and-paste techniques.
Instructions are given below for future reference.

> These instructions work for
> many word processors.

Pasting the contents of a WinBUGS window into a word-processor document

These instructions assume that both WinBUGS and your word processor are
running. The document in which you wish to insert WinBUGS input/output
should also be open.

◇   Select the contents of the WinBUGS document that is to be pasted into the
word-processor document (by highlighting it).

◇   Choose **Copy** from the **Edit** menu.

◇   Switch to your word processor.

> Alternatively, place the mouse
> pointer on your selection, click
> the right-hand mouse button,
> and choose **Copy** from the
> menu that is displayed (or press
> **Ctrl+C**).

◇ Place the cursor at the position in your document where you wish to insert the contents of the WinBUGS document.

◇ Choose **Paste** from the **Edit** menu of your word processor. The contents of the WinBUGS document will be inserted in your word-processor document.

Alternatively, press **Ctrl+V** to paste.

Note that if the WinBUGS compound document includes graphs as well as text, then you must paste the graphs and the text into the word-processor document separately.

At some stage, you may wish to print the contents of a WinBUGS document. Instructions for doing this are given below.

Printing a WinBUGS document

Printing the contents of a WinBUGS document (which may contain text and graphs) is straightforward. It is done as follows.

◇ Make the document window active (by clicking on it).

◇ Choose **Print...** from the **File** menu to obtain the **Print** dialogue box.

◇ Click on the **Print** button in the **Print** dialogue box to print the document.

Summary of Chapter 7

In this chapter, the stochastic simulation software package WinBUGS has been introduced. You have met several features of WinBUGS compound documents. In particular, you have learned how to open and close a compound document, and how to print a WinBUGS document. Some of the capabilities that WinBUGS possesses for word processing a document have been described briefly, and you have learned how to paste the contents of a WinBUGS compound document into a word-processor document.

Chapter 8
Model definition in WinBUGS

Before samples can be generated from a model using WinBUGS, the model must be written (defined) in the BUGS language. In this chapter, the BUGS language is introduced, and you will learn how to interpret the model definitions for standard distributions written in the language.

The definition of a normal distribution is described in Section 8.1, and the WinBUGS concept of nodes is introduced in Section 8.2. Definitions involving other standard distributions are discussed in Section 8.3.

8.1 Defining a model in WinBUGS

The main purpose of WinBUGS is to enable you to sample values from Bayesian posterior distributions. The sampled values can then be used for making inferences. In order to sample from a distribution, the statistical model needs to be defined (or 'coded') in a way that WinBUGS will understand. You will not be asked to do this: you will be given appropriate model definitions in WinBUGS compound documents. However, you will be expected to interpret them.

In WinBUGS, the BUGS language is used to define probability models.

Example 8.1 A model definition

Below is a distribution defined using the BUGS language.

```
model
{
    X ~ dnorm(10,0.125)
}
```

The symbol ~ is called a 'twiddle' by the developers of WinBUGS.

Notice that the definition consists of four lines of code. The first line, `model`, tells WinBUGS that the text within the curly brackets defines a model.

The third line, `X ~ dnorm(10,0.125)`, specifies that the random variable X has a normal distribution with mean 10 and variance 8 or, equivalently, that X has a normal distribution with mean 10 and precision $\frac{1}{8} = 0.125$. In other words,

$$X \sim N(10, 8).$$

The pair of brackets on lines 2 and 4 tells WinBUGS where the code for the model definition begins and ends.

Note the similarity between the mathematical notation for the model, $X \sim N(10, 8)$, and the BUGS definition of the model, `X ~ dnorm(10,0.125)`. In the BUGS language, the tilde character (~) means 'is distributed as' and corresponds to $\sim$ in mathematical notation. The term `dnorm(mu,tau)` means a normal probability density function (p.d.f.) with mean `mu` and *precision* `tau`. Note the use of the precision to specify the spread of a normal distribution. Elsewhere, normal distributions are usually defined using the variance, so care should be taken when interpreting WinBUGS code for a model involving a normal distribution. ◆

The probability density functions of other probability distributions are specified using their common names (or shortened versions thereof) preceded by `d` — for example, `dpois`, `dbin`, `dunif` and `dbeta`, for the Poisson, binomial, uniform and beta distributions, respectively. The parametrization that WinBUGS uses to specify a distribution is sometimes different from that used elsewhere: the normal and binomial distributions are the only distributions that you will meet in M249 for which this is the case.

8.2 Nodes

In WinBUGS, the random variables in a model, and any parameters for which a distribution is specified, are called **stochastic nodes**. There is a simple way of spotting a stochastic node in a model definition: a stochastic node is a quantity that is followed by the ~ symbol.

In WinBUGS, there are two other types of node — **constant nodes** and **deterministic nodes**. In model definitions, constant nodes and deterministic nodes are both quantities that are followed by the symbol `<-`. The notation `<-` can be read as 'takes the value'; it assigns to the quantity on its left-hand side the value defined on its right-hand side. A constant node is a parameter which takes a constant numerical value. Note that a function of a constant node is itself a constant node since it takes a constant numerical value. A deterministic node is a variable or parameter that is assigned a non-random value which is a function of other nodes. A deterministic node does *not* take a constant numerical value. However, the values it takes are determined by the values taken by other nodes. You will meet examples of all three types of nodes in this book.

Computer Activity 8.1   *Spotting nodes*

The model defined in Example 8.1 contains one node, the stochastic node X. This activity concerns the slightly more complicated model below.

```
model
{
    Y ~ dnorm(10,prec)
    prec <- 1/var
    var <- 8
}
```

This model definition refers to three nodes: Y, prec and var. For each node in this model, state whether it is a stochastic node, a constant node or a deterministic node.

The model considered in Computer Activity 8.1 says that Y has a normal distribution with mean 10 and precision prec, where prec is defined to be the reciprocal of var, and var takes the value 8. The use of two constant nodes allowed the parametrization of the normal distribution that BUGS uses to be converted into a more standard parametrization.

8.3   *WinBUGS commands for standard distributions*

The code for a Bayesian model may involve a variety of standard probability distributions. The standard distributions that you will be expected to recognize are listed in Table 8.1.

Table 8.1   Standard probability distributions and their WinBUGS commands

Distribution	BUGS command	Parameters
Poisson	X ~ dpois(a)	mean $a > 0$
Binomial	X ~ dbin(p,n)	success probability p, where $0 < p < 1$, number $n = 1, 2, \ldots$
Uniform	X ~ dunif(a,b)	a, b, where $a \leq X \leq b$
Normal	X ~ dnorm(mu,tau)	mean mu, $-\infty < mu < \infty$, precision tau > 0
Exponential	X ~ dexp(a)	$a > 0$, mean $= 1/a$
Gamma	X ~ dgamma(a,b)	shape $a > 0$, scale $b > 0$ (mean $= a/b$)
Beta	X ~ dbeta(a,b)	$a, b > 0$ (mean $= a/(a+b)$)

With the exception of the normal distribution, the parametrization that WinBUGS uses matches the parametrization that you have met elsewhere in M249. However, note that in the command for the binomial distribution, the first parameter is the probability of success p, not the number of trials n, as is usually the case.

WinBUGS uses efficient and accurate algorithms to sample from all these distributions. You need not be concerned with how WinBUGS does the sampling. You should focus on the modelling and analysis.

Computer Activity 8.2 *Reading WinBUGS model definitions*

For each of the model definitions below, write down the probability model to which it corresponds.

(a)
```
model
{
     X ~ dnorm(-5,0.5)
}
```

(b)
```
model
{
     X ~ dnorm(a,b)
     a <- 6
     b <- 5
}
```

(c)
```
model
{
     X ~ dbin(0.22,50)
}
```

(d)
```
model
{
     theta ~ dgamma(2.2,0.15)
}
```

Note that Greek letters cannot be used in the BUGS language, so the names of Greek letters are usually used instead.

(e)
```
model
{
     X ~ dpois(theta)
     theta ~ dgamma(5,1)
}
```

Summary of Chapter 8

In this chapter, the commands that WinBUGS uses to define some standard probability distributions have been introduced. You have seen how a simple probabilistic model is defined. In particular, you have learned that WinBUGS parametrizes a normal distribution by its mean and precision, rather than its mean and variance. You have also learned that WinBUGS calls all the variables and parameters in a model nodes, and that it categorizes nodes into three types — stochastic, deterministic and constant.

Chapter 9
Stochastic simulation from standard distributions

In this chapter, you will use WinBUGS to generate and analyse samples from a simple model relating to a standard probability distribution. The example that will be used concerns the ability of dogs to detect bladder cancer from the smell of a person's urine.

See Example 10.3 in *Book 4*.

The model that will be used relates to θ_1, the proportion of samples identified correctly by dogs trained with fresh urine. In *Book 4*, you saw that for a

Beta$(1,1)$ prior and the observed data, the posterior for θ_1 is Beta$(19,19)$. The corresponding model definition written in BUGS code is in the compound document **dogs1.odc**.

In Section 9.1, you will use WinBUGS to generate some samples from the posterior distribution for θ_1; and in Section 9.2, you will use WinBUGS to summarize these samples, both graphically and numerically. You will need the results of Computer Activity 9.1 for Computer Activity 9.2, so you should work through these two activities in one computer session.

9.1 Generating samples in WinBUGS

Using WinBUGS to generate samples from a model involves several steps. These are listed in the following box.

> **Generating samples in WinBUGS**
>
> Step 1:   Write the model definition in the BUGS language.
>
> Step 2:   Check the model definition using WinBUGS.
>
> Step 3:   Compile the model. WinBUGS will translate the model definition from the BUGS language into the form it needs internally.
>
> Step 4:   Specify initial values.
>
> Step 5:   Specify which nodes (stochastic or deterministic) to monitor. That is, specify the random variables or parameters for which the sampled values are to be stored. Although samples will be generated for the other nodes, they will not be stored, so they will not be available to analyse.
>
> Step 6:   Generate a specified number of samples from the model.

You will not be expected to do step 1 in M249. You will be given the model definition written in the BUGS language.

Steps 2 to 6 are illustrated in Computer Activity 9.1.

Computer Activity 9.1   Generating samples from Beta(19,19)

In this activity, you will perform steps 2 to 6 for the model

$$\theta_1 \sim \text{Beta}(19,19).$$

Start WinBUGS, and open the compound document **dogs1.odc**. This contains the definition of the beta model $\theta_1 \sim \text{Beta}(19,19)$.

File > Open...

Step 2: Check the model

Checking the model means using WinBUGS to check that the model definition obeys all BUGS language rules ('syntax'). In M249, you will be given correct model definitions. Nevertheless, WinBUGS requires you to check the model definition before generating the samples. Do this now, as follows.

Checking the model does *not* ensure that the model definition corresponds to the intended model.

◇   Highlight the word `model` in the WinBUGS document.

◇   Choose **Specification...** from the **Model** menu to obtain the **Specification Tool** dialogue box.

The highlighting of the word `model` will change from black to white, but nevertheless the word is still 'highlighted'.

◇   Click on **check model** in the **Specification Tool** dialogue box. WinBUGS will check the model definition.

◇   A message box warning that `the new model will replace the old one` may appear. If so, then click on **OK** in the box.

The message `model is syntactically correct` will appear in the status bar at the bottom of the main WinBUGS window. This means that WinBUGS has checked that the BUGS code defines a valid model.

You will find it convenient to leave the **Specification Tool** dialogue box open throughout your WinBUGS session.

Step 3: Compile the model

Compile the model, as follows.

◇ Click on **compile** in the **Specification Tool** dialogue box.

The message `model compiled` will appear in the status bar, indicating that WinBUGS has done the necessary internal translation of the model definition.

Step 4: Specify initial values

WinBUGS uses initial values to start the simulation process. Initial values are required for all of the stochastic nodes in the model. In this example, there is one stochastic node, `theta1`, so one initial value is needed.

There are two options for specifying initial values. You can specify the initial values yourself, or you can get WinBUGS to simulate initial values from the model.

For the model $\theta_1 \sim \text{Beta}(19, 19)$, the initial value for θ_1 does not influence later simulated values since independent values will be generated from a standard probability distribution. Therefore let WinBUGS generate the initial value for `theta1`, as follows.

◇ Click on **gen inits** in the **Specification Tool** dialogue box. WinBUGS will generate an initial value of θ_1. For this model, the initial value will be sampled directly from the Beta$(19, 19)$ distribution.

The status bar will display the message `initial values generated, model initialized`.

Step 5: Specify nodes to monitor

WinBUGS generates sample values for all nodes whose values are not constant. However, these values are not stored automatically. Therefore you must tell WinBUGS the nodes for which you wish to have samples available to summarize or analyse. That is, you must tell WinBUGS the name(s) of the node(s) you wish to *monitor*.

For the model $\theta_1 \sim \text{Beta}(19, 19)$, there is one stochastic node, `theta1`. Specify the node `theta1` for monitoring, as follows.

◇ Choose **Samples...** from the **Inference** menu to obtain the **Sample Monitor Tool** dialogue box.

◇ Type `theta1` in the **node** field in the **Sample Monitor Tool** dialogue box, then click on **set**.

You will find it convenient to have the **Sample Monitor Tool** dialogue box open throughout your WinBUGS session.

Step 6: Generate the sample

Having defined, checked and compiled the model, generated initial values and specified which nodes to monitor, you are ready to generate the sample.

In general, the larger the sample size used, the more accurate inferences will be. For now, a sample of size 1000 will suffice but, in future, you may need to take larger samples than this. Generate a sample of size 1000, as follows.

◇ Choose **Update...** from the **Model** menu to obtain the **Update Tool** dialogue box. (You will find it convenient to leave the **Update Tool** dialogue box open throughout your WinBUGS session.)

◇ The entry in the **updates** field indicates that the default sample size is $N = 1000$. Hence you should leave this default sample size, and all the other entries in this dialogue box, unchanged.

◇ Click on **update** in the **Update Tool** dialogue box.

Notice that the entry in the **iteration** field of the **Update Tool** dialogue box indicates the number of simulated values as they are generated. The simulation of

Margin notes

You may find it helpful to move the **Specification Tool** dialogue box so that it does not obscure the main WinBUGS window. To do this, place the mouse pointer on the title bar, then hold down the mouse button while you drag the dialogue box to a more convenient position.

For some models, careful choice of initial values is important.

Recall that WinBUGS calls all the quantities in a model *nodes*.

You may find it helpful to move the **Sample Monitor Tool** dialogue box so that it does not obscure the main WinBUGS window or the **Specification Tool** dialogue box.

You may find it helpful to move the **Update Tool** dialogue box so that it does not obscure the main WinBUGS window or the other two dialogue boxes.

WinBUGS uses the term *update*. You can think of this as being synonymous with *sample*, *simulate* or *generate*.

1000 values of θ_1 is extremely quick (unless you are running WinBUGS on a slow computer) and thus you might have missed this. The status bar provides a message telling you how long the simulation took in seconds; for this simulation, it will probably say `updates took 0 s`.

This means that the simulation took less than one second.

The simulation is now complete. Do not exit WinBUGS. If you do, then the generated sample of values for θ_1 will be lost and you will have to repeat this activity before you can complete Computer Activity 9.2.

9.2 Analysing samples in WinBUGS

Having generated a sample in WinBUGS, WinBUGS can be used to analyse the sample by producing graphical and numerical summaries of the simulated values. In this section, you will explore some of available methods. The methods described are accessed via the **Sample Monitor Tool** dialogue box.

Computer Activity 9.2   *Producing summaries*

In Computer Activity 9.1, you generated a sample of size 1000 for the parameter θ_1, where $\theta_1 \sim \text{Beta}(19, 19)$. In this activity, you will produce graphical and numerical summaries of this sample.

The main graphical summary in WinBUGS is an estimate of the probability density function of a random variable or parameter. For continuous variables, WinBUGS produces what is called a **kernel density estimate**. A kernel density estimate can be interpreted as a continuous 'smoothed' version of a histogram. (You do not need to know how a kernel density estimate is constructed, only how it can be interpreted.) Numerical summaries largely consist of the mean, the standard deviation and various quantiles. These summaries are obtained using the **Sample Monitor Tool** dialogue box, as follows.

◇ Obtain the **Sample Monitor Tool** dialogue box, if it is not already open.

Inference > Samples...

◇ Click on the down-pointing arrowhead to the right of the **node** field (which is currently empty). A drop-down list of all the variables in the model that you specified to be monitored will be displayed.

◇ Select `theta1` from the drop-down list (by clicking on its name). The word `theta1` will appear in the **node** field, and the ten buttons in the dialogue box will become active. This indicates that you can now obtain summaries, both graphical and numerical, of the node `theta1`.

◇ Click on **density** in the **Sample Monitor Tool** dialogue box. A window entitled **Kernel density** will appear containing a graphical representation of the posterior p.d.f. for θ_1 based on the sampled values. The contents of this window are shown in Figure 9.1.

The window in which the kernel density estimate appears is a WinBUGS compound document.

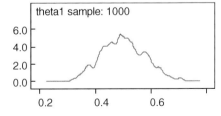

Figure 9.1   Kernel density estimate of the posterior p.d.f. for θ_1 based on 1000 sampled values

◇ Click on **stats** in the **Sample Monitor Tool** dialogue box. A window entitled **Node statistics** will appear. The contents of this window are reproduced overleaf.

Your graphical and numerical summaries may look slightly different from those given here, but they should be broadly similar.

node	mean	sd	MC error	2.5%	median	97.5%	start	sample
theta1	0.5009	0.07874	0.002468	0.3574	0.4976	0.659	1	1000

The kernel density estimate in Figure 9.1 shows that the posterior for θ_1 is roughly symmetric around a central value of 0.5, with values between 0.4 and 0.6 being most likely. As an estimate of the true Beta(19, 19) p.d.f., the kernel density estimate is rather poor since it is far from smooth. Nevertheless, it represents reasonably well the main features of the distribution for θ_1, such as its location, dispersion and skewness. A better — that is, smoother — appearance can be obtained by taking a larger sample of values.

This lack of smoothness is a feature of the kernel density estimates produced by WinBUGS, not of kernel density estimates in general.

The **Node statistics** window contains summary statistics and other information about the sampled values for theta1. Most of the entries should be self-explanatory. The items in the window are described briefly in Table 9.1. In this table, x_i denotes the ith sampled value of node x.

Table 9.1 Columns in the **Node statistics** window

Column	Contents
node	the name of the random variable or parameter that is being summarized
mean	the sample mean, $\bar{x}$, of the simulated values used in the calculation, where $$\bar{x} = \frac{1}{N} \sum_{i=\text{start}}^{N+\text{start}} x_i$$
sd	the standard deviation of the sampled values, calculated using the formula $$\text{sd} = \sqrt{\frac{1}{N} \sum_{i=\text{start}}^{N+\text{start}} (x_i - \bar{x})^2}$$
MC error	the Monte Carlo standard error of the mean
2.5%	the sample 0.025-quantile of the simulated values
median	the sample median (or sample 0.5-quantile) of the simulated values
97.5%	the sample 0.975-quantile of the simulated values
start	the simulated values from x_{start} onwards are analysed
sample	N, the number of sampled values used in the calculations

Note that the divisor in the formula for the standard deviation is N rather than $N - 1$. For the large samples commonly generated in WinBUGS, the two versions of the standard deviation give very similar estimates, so any differences can be ignored. Estimates of the posterior mean and standard deviation of θ_1 are provided by the sample mean and sample standard deviation, 0.5009 and 0.078 74, respectively. These values are similar to, but not the same as, those reported in Example 11.2 of *Book 4*, which were based on a different simulation of 1000 values.

The Monte Carlo standard error (MC error) gives a measure of the accuracy of the sample mean estimate. Therefore it is good practice to report the MC error in brackets after a mean estimate. The estimate of the MC error provided by WinBUGS can be used to assess whether the sample size is adequate.

WinBUGS reports the sample 0.025-quantile, 0.5-quantile and 0.975-quantile by default. Usually these are the quantiles of most interest. The 0.025-quantile and the 0.975-quantile can be used to give an estimate of the equal-tailed 95% credible interval for the quantity of interest. In this case, the estimated credible interval for θ_1 is (0.3574, 0.6590). WinBUGS uses the terminology 'percentile' rather than quantile: for example, the 0.025-quantile is the 2.5th percentile. Some other quantiles can be obtained by selecting them in the **percentiles** area of the **Sample Monitor Tool** dialogue box before clicking on **stats**.

In general, the $100q$th percentile is the q-quantile.

Suppose that you are interested in an equal-tailed 90% credible interval for θ_1. The limits of such an interval can be estimated by the sample 0.05-quantile and the sample 0.95-quantile (that is, the 5th and 95th percentiles). Obtain these quantiles now, as follows.

◇   In the **Sample Monitor Tool** dialogue box, click on 5 in the **percentiles** area: the value 5 will be highlighted.

◇   Hold down the **Ctrl** key on your keyboard and click on 95 in the **percentiles** area: the value 95 will be highlighted.

◇   Click on the **stats** button in the **Sample Monitor Tool** dialogue box.

Another **Node statistics** window will open, which includes the 0.05-quantile and 0.95-quantile. The contents of this window are reproduced below.

node	mean	sd	MC error	5.0%	95.0%	start	sample
theta1	0.5009	0.07874	0.002468	0.3743	0.635	1	1000

The estimate of the equal-tailed 90% credible interval for θ_1 is $(0.3743, 0.6350)$. Notice that this interval is narrower than the 95% credible interval, as expected.

Notice that the numerical summaries produced by WinBUGS are displayed to four significant figures. (When the last significant figure is 0, it is not displayed.) However, four-figure accuracy is seldom required, so from now on, for the most part, results will be reported to three significant figures.

The following box contains a summary of the steps involved in using WinBUGS to sample from a model and analyse the sample.

Model specification, simulation and analysis

1   In WinBUGS, open the file containing the model definition written in the BUGS language.   File > **Open...**

2   Check the model definition in WinBUGS.

   ◇   Highlight the word `model` in the file containing the model definition.

   ◇   In the **Specification Tool** dialogue box, click on **check model**.   Model > **Specification...**

3   Compile the model.

   ◇   In the **Specification Tool** dialogue box, click on **compile**.

4   Generate initial values.

   ◇   Click on **gen inits** in the **Specification Tool** dialogue box.

5   Specify nodes to monitor.

   ◇   In the **Sample Monitor Tool** dialogue box, for each variable or   Inference > **Samples...**
parameter about which you wish to make inferences, type its name in the **node** field, then click on **set**.

6   Generate samples.

   ◇   In the **Update Tool** dialogue box, enter the required sample size in   Model > **Update...**
the **updates** field, then click on the **update** button.

7   Analyse samples.

   ◇   Select the variable(s) or parameter(s) of interest from the drop-down list in the **Sample Monitor Tool** dialogue box.

   ◇   Click on the **density** button in the **Sample Monitor Tool** dialogue box. This generates a graphical estimate of the distribution of the variable(s) and parameter(s).

   ◇   Click on the **stats** button in the **Sample Monitor Tool** dialogue box. This generates numerical summaries of the variable(s) and parameter(s) of interest.

If at any stage you make a mistake, then simply go back to step 2 and start the procedure again.

Computer Activity 9.3   *Another beta distribution*

In the experiment to investigate whether or not dogs can detect bladder cancer from the smell of a sample of urine, some of the dogs were trained using dried urine. This activity concerns θ_2, the proportion of samples identified correctly by dogs trained using dried urine. For a Beta$(1,1)$ prior and the observed data, the posterior for θ_2 is Beta$(5, 15)$. You will generate a sample of values from this distribution, and analyse the sample.

See Example 10.3 of *Book 4*.

(a) Open the WinBUGS document **dogs2.odc**. Satisfy yourself that the model definition given in this file corresponds to the model $\theta_2 \sim$ Beta$(5, 15)$.

(b) In WinBUGS, check this model definition.

(c) Compile the model.

(d) Generate an initial value for θ_2.

(e) Tell WinBUGS to monitor θ_2.

(f) Use WinBUGS to sample $N = 1000$ values from the posterior distribution for θ_2.

(g) Use the sample to obtain an estimate of the posterior p.d.f. for θ_2. Based on this density estimate, what is the most likely (posterior) value of θ_2?

(h) Report estimates of the posterior mean and standard deviation, and of the equal-tailed 95% and the equal-tailed 90% credible intervals for θ_2 based on the simulated values.

(i) In each experiment, one urine sample out of seven was from a patient with bladder cancer. From your results, does it appear that the dogs identify the urine sample from the patient with bladder cancer correctly by chance alone?

If at any stage you are presented with an error message, go back to part (b) (step 2).

Summary of Chapter 9

In this chapter, you have used WinBUGS to sample values from models which are standard probability distributions, and to summarize the sampled values using graphical and numerical summaries. You have learned how to obtain sample quantiles (percentiles) other than the WinBUGS default quantiles.

Chapter 10
Transformations and multivariate problems

In this chapter, you will use WinBUGS to generate and analyse samples from models that are slightly more complicated than those considered in Chapter 9. In Section 10.1, the situation where the quantity of interest is a function of a parameter that has a standard distribution is discussed. In Section 10.2, you will use WinBUGS to simulate from two multi-parameter posterior distributions, and to explore the relationships between the sampled values for the different parameters.

10.1   Transformations of parameters

In Chapter 9, you learned how to simulate values from the posterior for θ when θ is a parameter with a standard probability distribution. Sampling from the distribution of a transformation $g(\theta)$ of θ is also straightforward: simply sample values of θ, then apply the function g to the sampled values. This is illustrated in Computer Activity 10.1.

Computer Activity 10.1   The sex ratio of births in the UK

The analysis of data on the numbers of male births and female births in Milton Keynes, UK, in 2001 was discussed in Example 13.1 of *Book 4*. The proportion of male births in the UK was denoted θ. You saw that with a Beta$(5, 5)$ prior for θ, the posterior for θ, based on the sample of data from Milton Keynes, is Beta$(1447, 1393)$; that is,

$\theta|\text{data} \sim \text{Beta}(1447, 1393).$

This is a standard probability distribution from which it is easy to simulate. However, interest lies mainly in the posterior distribution for $\phi = \theta/(1 - \theta)$, the so-called 'sex ratio'. In the BUGS language, the model for θ and ϕ is as follows.

```
model
{
    theta ~ dbeta(1447,1393)
    phi <- theta/(1-theta)
}
```

Here, `phi` is a deterministic node, which applies the transformation `theta/(1-theta)` to the stochastic node `theta`. Adding this line to the model specification makes it possible to simulate values of $\phi = \theta/(1 - \theta)$ directly in WinBUGS.

Suppose that $N = 10\,000$ values are to be simulated from this model — that is, $10\,000$ values for each of `theta` and `phi`. Note that the model specification tells WinBUGS that each time a value of `theta` is generated from the Beta$(1447, 1393)$ distribution, this value is to be transformed to give a value of `phi`. Hence a simulation from the posterior distributions for both θ and ϕ will be obtained.

The procedure for generating a sample of values from the posterior distributions for θ and ϕ is essentially the same as that described in Chapter 9. The model definition is in the WinBUGS document **mkbirths.odc**.

Start WinBUGS, or if it is already running, close it and restart it, then open the file.

Simulate $10\,000$ values from the posterior distributions for θ and ϕ, as follows.

◇   Check the model in WinBUGS. (Highlight the word `model` in the file **mkbirths.odc**, then click on **check** in the **Specification Tool** dialogue box.)

◇   Compile the model. (Click on **compile** in the **Specification Tool** dialogue box.)

◇   Specify the initial values. For this model, the initial values are not important, so let WinBUGS generate the initial values: click on **gen inits** in the **Specification Tool** dialogue box.

◇   Specify the nodes to monitor. In this example, both θ and ϕ are of interest so, in the **Sample Monitor Tool** dialogue box, type `theta` in the **node** field and click on the **set** button, then type `phi` in the **node** field and click on the **set** button.

◇   A sample of $10\,000$ values is required so, in the **Update Tool** dialogue box, add an extra 0 to the end of the value 1000 in the **updates** field. This sets the value of **updates** to 10000. Do not click on **update** for the moment.

Restarting WinBUGS resets the default percentiles in the **Sample Monitor Tool** dialogue box.

Model > Specification...

Inference > Samples...

Model > Update...

As it stands, this simulation would take several seconds to run, because the value in the **refresh** field is a small proportion of the value in the **updates** field. The value of **refresh** indicates how often, in terms of the number of values sampled, output on the screen should be updated. If the value of **refresh** is small, then your computer will spend more time updating the screen than doing the sampling, thus slowing down the simulation. This problem can be overcome by increasing the value of **refresh**.

◇ In the **Update Tool** dialogue box, change the value in the **refresh** field to 1000.

This is a good idea when performing *very* large simulations.

◇ Now click on **update**. WinBUGS will generate the sample. (This should be very quick.)

The time taken for the simulation will depend on your computer.

Although interest lies primarily in the sampled values of the sex ratio ϕ, it is also worth looking at the sampled values of θ. Analyse the sampled values, as follows.

◇ In the **Sample Monitor Tool** dialogue box, type an asterisk, *, in the **node** field. This tells WinBUGS to produce summaries for all the nodes that it has been told to monitor — in this example, `theta` and `phi`.

◇ Click on **density** in the **Sample Monitor Tool** dialogue box to produce kernel density estimates for θ and ϕ.

◇ Click on **stats** in the **Sample Monitor Tool** dialogue box to obtain numerical summaries for the two quantities.

Your density estimates should be similar to those in Figure 10.1.

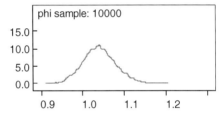
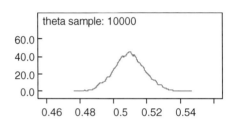

Figure 10.1   Kernel density estimates of the posterior p.d.f.s for ϕ and θ

The density estimate for ϕ represents an estimate of the posterior p.d.f. for the sex ratio.

The summary statistics in the **Node statistics** window are reproduced below.

Your values may be different to these, but they should be broadly similar.

node	mean	sd	MC error	2.5%	median	97.5%	start	sample
phi	1.04	0.03891	3.962E-4	0.9658	1.039	1.12	1	10000
theta	0.5096	0.00934	9.501E-5	0.4913	0.5095	0.5283	1	10000

From these summaries, estimates of the posterior mean (MC error), median and standard deviation, and the equal-tailed 95% credible interval for ϕ are 1.04 (0.000 396), 1.039, 0.0389 and (0.966, 1.12), respectively. These summaries are similar to the values reported in Example 13.1 of *Book 4*.

WinBUGS can handle many of the standard mathematical functions that are used in transformations of parameters, such as $\log x$, e^x and $\sqrt{x}$. A list of some of the most common functions is given in Table 10.1.

Table 10.1   Common functions and their WinBUGS syntax

WinBUGS syntax	Description
`abs(x)`	the absolute value of x
`cos(x)`	the cosine of x
`equals(x,y)`	returns 1 if $x = y$ and 0 otherwise
`exp(x)`	the exponential function e^x
`log(x)`	the natural logarithm function $\log x$
`pow(x,y)`	the power function x^y
`sin(x)`	the sine of x
`sqrt(x)`	the square root of x

Computer Activity 10.2   The log odds for a male birth

The odds for a male birth is the proportion of male births divided by the proportion of non-male births. That is,

$$\text{odds} = \frac{\theta}{1-\theta}.$$

This is the sex ratio ϕ that you estimated in Computer Activity 10.1. Odds are quite often expressed on a logarithmic scale. The log odds is defined as follows:

$$\log \text{odds} = \log\left(\frac{\theta}{1-\theta}\right).$$

In this activity, you will use WinBUGS to sample from the posterior distribution for the log odds for a male birth, and use the sampled values to make inferences about the log odds.

(a) In WinBUGS, open the file **mkbirths2.odc**. What name has been given to the node which corresponds to the log odds?

(b) Sample $N = 10\,000$ values from this model. In other words, check the model, compile the model, generate some initial values and specify that the node corresponding to the log odds is to be monitored, then generate the values.

(c) Use the sample that you generated in part (b) to produce an estimate of the posterior p.d.f. for the log odds for a male birth, and report estimates of the posterior mean and standard deviation, and the equal-tailed 95% credible interval for the log odds.

(d) Comment informally on $P(\log \text{odds} < 0)$.

10.2   Multivariate problems

So far, you have used WinBUGS to obtain samples from models that are standard univariate distributions. In WinBUGS, this corresponds to models that have one stochastic node. In this section, you will use WinBUGS to simulate from multivariate posterior distributions. Such models have two or more stochastic nodes. You will also see how relationships between sampled values for different parameters can be displayed and analysed.

Computer Activity 10.3 Normal model with unknown mean and variance

In Section 14 of *Book 4*, the problem of estimating the density of the Earth based on Henry Cavendish's measurements of 1798 was discussed. The model used for Cavendish's data was normal with unknown mean μ and unknown precision τ:

$$X \sim N(\mu, 1/\tau).$$

The following normal-gamma conjugate prior for the mean μ and precision τ was adopted:

$$\mu|\tau \sim N(4, 7/\tau),$$
$$\tau \sim \text{Gamma}(2.2, 0.15).$$

See Example 14.2 of *Book 4*.

This was combined with Cavendish's data to obtain the normal-gamma posterior for μ and τ with components

$$\mu|\tau, \text{data} \sim N(5.44, 0.0343/\tau),$$
$$\tau|\text{data} \sim \text{Gamma}(16.7, 0.982).$$

See Example 14.3 of *Book 4*.

In this activity, you will use WinBUGS to sample 1000 values of μ and 1000 values of τ from this posterior distribution. Notice that τ has a standard distribution, and once τ is known, μ also has a standard distribution. This model is defined in the file **cavposterior.odc**. Open this file in WinBUGS. The file contains the following model definition.

```
model
{
    mu ~ dnorm(5.44,prec)
    prec <- tau/0.0343
    tau ~ dgamma(16.7,0.982)
}
```

There are two stochastic nodes in this model definition, `mu` and `tau`, and one deterministic node, `prec`. Also, the precision of `mu` depends on `tau` via the deterministic node `prec`.

Obtain a sample of 1000 pairs of values, as follows.

◇ In WinBUGS, check and compile this model (by clicking on **check model** and then **compile** in the **Specification Tool** dialogue box).

◇ Obtain initial values for the nodes `mu` and `tau`: let WinBUGS generate the initial values. (Click on **gen inits** in the **Specification Tool** dialogue box.)

◇ In this activity, the distributions of `mu` and `tau` are of interest, but not `prec`. In the **Sample Monitor Tool** dialogue box, type `mu` in the **node** field and click on **set**, then type `tau` in the **node** field and click on **set**.

◇ In the **Update Tool** dialogue box, make sure that the value in the **updates** field is 1000. Click on **update**.

The relationship between two quantities can be explored using scatterplots and correlations. In WinBUGS, scatterplots and correlations can be produced for two (or more) monitored nodes. Obtain a scatterplot of the simulated values of μ and τ and the corresponding correlation coefficient, as follows.

◇ Choose **Correlations** from the **Inference** menu. The **Correlation Tool** dialogue box will open.

◇ There are two empty **nodes** fields at the top of the dialogue box. Type `tau` in the left-hand field and `mu` in the right-hand field. These entries specify the variables to plot on the horizontal axis and the vertical axis of a bivariate scatterplot, respectively.

◇ Click on **scatter** in the **Correlation Tool** dialogue box to produce the scatterplot.

◇ Click on **print** in the **Correlation Tool** dialogue box. This provides an estimate of the posterior correlation between the two parameters.

Clicking on **print** here will *not* cause anything to be printed on your printer.

The scatterplot will be displayed in a window entitled **Bivariate posterior scatterplot**, and the correlation between the sampled values of μ and τ will be given in a window entitled **Pairwise correlations**. The scatterplot is shown in Figure 10.2.

The scatterplot shows the posterior relationship between the two parameters. The points form a triangular pattern. The range of values of τ is largest (roughly between 10 and 40) for values of μ in the range 5.4 to 5.5. For smaller and larger values of μ, the range of values of τ tends to be smaller. So the two parameters appear to be dependent.

The scatterplot also suggests that the two parameters are not linearly related. This is confirmed by the correlation coefficient between the sampled values of μ and τ, which is given in the **Pairwise correlations** window: the correlation is 0.125, a value which is fairly close to zero. This demonstrates that dependence and correlation are not the same.

In this example, the marginal posterior distribution for μ, the density of the Earth, is of primary interest. Obtain summaries of the marginal distributions for μ and τ, as follows. (The method is the same as that used in Computer Activities 10.1 and 10.2.)

◇   In the **Sample Monitor Tool** dialogue box, type an asterisk, *, in the **node** field.

◇   Click on the **density** and **stats** buttons in the **Sample Monitor Tool** dialogue box.

The left-hand diagram in the **Kernel density** window gives an estimate of the density of $f(\mu|\text{data})$; it is reproduced in Figure 10.3.

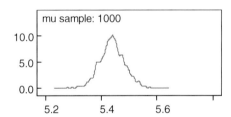

Figure 10.3   Kernel density estimate of the marginal posterior distribution for μ

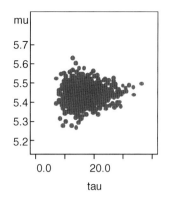

Figure 10.2   Scatterplot of simulated values from the joint posterior distribution for μ and τ

This diagram encapsulates all the available information about the value of μ, the true density of the Earth, whilst allowing for uncertainty about the value of τ.

The numerical summaries of the two marginal posterior distributions, as shown in the WinBUGS output, are reproduced below.

node	mean	sd	MC error	2.5%	median	97.5%	start	sample
mu	5.44	0.04675	0.001279	5.351	5.44	5.535	1	1000
tau	17.03	4.394	0.1464	9.465	16.62	27.31	1	1000

Based on the 1000 sampled values, an estimate of the posterior mean for μ is 5.44 (0.001 28), and an estimate of the equal-tailed 95% credible interval for μ is $(5.351, 5.535)$.

Computer Activity 10.4   *Difference between binomial proportions*

In Example 13.2 of *Book 4*, simulation from the posterior distribution for the difference between two binomial proportions was discussed.

The quantity of interest was $d = \theta_1 - \theta_2$, where θ_1 and θ_2 denote the proportions of urine samples identified correctly by dogs trained using fresh urine and by dogs trained using dried urine, respectively. Thus the distribution of d depends on the joint posterior distribution for θ_1 and θ_2. In this example, the joint posterior distribution for θ_1 and θ_2 can be written as two independent posterior distributions:

$$\theta_1|\text{data} \sim \text{Beta}(19, 19), \quad \theta_2|\text{data} \sim \text{Beta}(5, 15).$$

In this activity, you will use WinBUGS to generate samples from the joint posterior distribution for θ_1 and θ_2, and hence obtain samples from the posterior distribution for d, and to make inferences about the posterior distribution for d based on these samples.

(a) In WinBUGS, open the file **diffdogs.odc**. Verify that the model definition in this file corresponds to the model above.

(b) Check and compile this model. Get WinBUGS to generate all necessary initial values, then specify that only the parameter d is to be monitored, and generate 10 000 sample values from the posterior distribution for d.

(c) Summarize the posterior distribution for d by means of a kernel density estimate, and report estimates of the posterior mean and the equal-tailed 95% credible interval for d. Does it appear to matter what type of urine was used to train the dogs?

Summary of Chapter 10

In this chapter, you have learned how to deal with transformations of parameters in WinBUGS. You have also used WinBUGS to simulate from a posterior distribution involving two parameters, to produce a scatterplot of the simulated values, and to obtain an estimate of the correlation between the two parameters. You have also learned how to generate samples from the posterior distribution for the difference between two binomial proportions.

Chapter 11
MCMC in WinBUGS

In Chapters 9 and 10, you used WinBUGS to simulate from standard probability distributions in order to make inferences about parameters in a Bayesian model. WinBUGS sampled directly from the distributions and produced a sequence of independent samples. However, the real power of WinBUGS is its ability to sample from non-standard posterior distributions. It uses Markov chain Monte Carlo (MCMC) to do this.

In this chapter, the posterior distribution will be specified in terms of the likelihood and the prior, and MCMC will be used to obtain samples. The procedure for dealing with samples obtained using MCMC is similar to that used in Chapters 9 and 10 for Monte Carlo samples. The only difference is that inference is based only on iterations after the sequence of sampled values has settled down.

The use of WinBUGS to generate samples using MCMC and to analyse the sampled values will be illustrated using the 29 experimental measurements of the density of the Earth made at the end of the 18th century by the scientist Henry Cavendish. These 29 measurements were introduced in Section 14 of *Book 4*.

In Computer Activity 10.3, you sampled from the posterior distribution of a conjugate model for the data. In this chapter, independent prior distributions will be used, as described in Example 16.3 of *Book 4*. As before, the model for the data is the normal model

$$X \sim N(\mu, 1/\tau).$$

However, the following independent prior distributions for the unknown mean and precision will be used:

$$\mu \sim N(4, 1),$$
$$\tau \sim \text{Gamma}(2.2, 0.15).$$

It is difficult to obtain an explicit mathematical formula for the posterior joint density for μ and τ, so MCMC will be used to obtain samples.

You should try to work through all the activities in this chapter in one computer session, as they are linked.

Computer Activity 11.1   Generating samples using MCMC

Start WinBUGS, and open the file **nonconjnormal.odc**.

This file contains the model definition. Notice that both the model for the data and the priors appear explicitly in this model definition. There is no need to work out the posterior before attempting to sample from it.

The model for the data is specified using a `for` loop. Curly brackets, { and }, enclose the central part of the loop, which is as follows.

```
x[i] ~ dnorm(mu,tau)
```

The `for` loop tells WinBUGS to do whatever is in the central part of the loop for `i=1`, then again for `i=2`, up to `i=n`. This `for` loop is translated as 'for i in the range $1, 2, \ldots, n$, let x_i be an observation from a normal distribution with mean μ and precision τ'.

◇   Check the model definition in WinBUGS, but do *not* compile the model yet. The WinBUGS status bar should report that the `model is syntactically correct`.

Cavendish's data comprise 29 measurements. In the model, the values of $x_1, \ldots, x_{29}$ are defined as stochastic nodes. In all the models that you sampled from using WinBUGS in Chapters 9 and 10, the values of any stochastic nodes were not known. However, in this example, the values of $x_1, \ldots, x_{29}$ are known: their values have been observed (by Cavendish originally). Only the parameters of the model for $x_1, \ldots, x_{29}$ are not known in advance.

To ensure that WinBUGS does not sample new values for $x_1, \ldots, x_{29}$, the values for these stochastic nodes will be loaded into WinBUGS as data. Notice also that in the model definition, n is used to denote the number of observations, yet a value for n is not given in the model. So this constant, n, must also be loaded into WinBUGS as part of the data.

The data are in the file **cavendish.odc**. Load the data now, as follows.

◇ In WinBUGS, open the compound document **cavendish.odc**. The data are in a form that WinBUGS will recognize.

◇ Highlight the word `list` in the file **cavendish.odc**.

◇ Click on **load data** in the **Specification Tool** dialogue box. The message `data loaded` will appear in the status bar. This indicates that the data have been loaded successfully.

Now generate samples of values of μ and τ, as follows.

◇ Compile the model by clicking on **compile** in the **Specification Tool** dialogue box.

◇ Click on **gen inits** in the **Specification Tool** dialogue box, and WinBUGS will generate initial values.

◇ Specify μ and τ to be monitored: enter `mu` in the **node** field of the **Sample Monitor Tool** dialogue box and click on **set**, then enter `tau` in the **node** field and click on **set**.

◇ Generate 1000 samples of `mu` and `tau`: enter `1000` in the **updates** field of the **Update Tool** dialogue box and click on **update**.

> In M249, any data you need to use with WinBUGS will be given to you in an appropriate format.
>
> Model > Specification...
>
> Inference > Samples...
>
> Model > Update...

In Chapters 9 and 10, WinBUGS sampled from the posterior distributions directly. Thus all the simulated values were independent samples from the posterior distribution, and all the values could be used for inference.

When the posterior distribution is defined in terms of the likelihood and the prior, WinBUGS uses MCMC to generate the samples. When samples are generated using MCMC, they are not independent. Moreover, only samples obtained after the sampled values have settled down so that they appear to be from the equilibrium distribution can be treated as samples from the posterior distribution. Samples obtained before this point should not be included in any graphical and numerical summaries. When MCMC is used to generate samples, the point at which convergence appears to have occurred must be assessed, and samples obtained before this point must be discarded.

Computer Activity 11.2   Checking convergence

In this activity, you will investigate whether it is reasonable to assume that the sampled values obtained in Computer Activity 11.1 have converged by iteration 100. You will do this by inspecting trace plots of `mu` and `tau`.

If the transient phase lasts for no more than 100 iterations, then all samples obtained after iteration 100 will appear to have come from the equilibrium distribution. The distribution of samples before this point is not important. Thus the trace plots need display only iterations 101 onwards.

Obtain trace plots of `mu` and `tau`, as follows.

◇ In the **Sample Monitor Tool** dialogue box, type an asterisk, `*`, in the **node** field to select all monitored nodes (`mu` and `tau` in this case).

◇ Enter `101` in the **beg** field in the **Sample Monitor Tool** dialogue box, and check that the value in the **end** field is at least `1000`. Results for iteration 101 onward will be used in the subsequent analysis.

◇ In the **Sample Monitor Tool** dialogue box, click on **history**.

> The values **beg** and **end** denote the first and last iterations that are used in the subsequent analysis.

Trace plots for `mu` and `tau`, for iterations 101 onwards, will be displayed in a window entitled **Time series**. These are reproduced in Figure 11.1.

> Your plot may look slightly different, but it should be broadly similar to Figure 11.1.

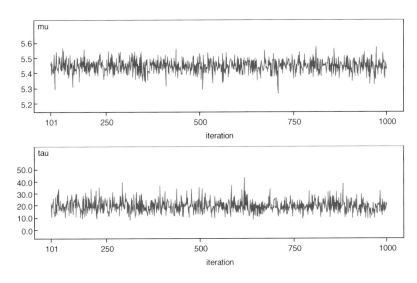

Figure 11.1   Trace plots of simulated values of μ and τ, ignoring the first 100 iterations

The values appear to come from a distribution with constant mean and variance. So these plots do not provide any evidence that the sequence of values has not converged by iteration 101, and hence the values can be treated as samples from the equilibrium distribution.

Note that there is a **trace** button in the **Sample Monitor Tool** dialogue box. This provides a *dynamic* trace plot of the simulated values, that is, the plot is re-drawn after every **refresh** iterations as the simulation progresses (where **refresh** is the value in the **Update Tool** dialogue box). This is in contrast to **history** which, as its name suggests, shows the trace of the simulated values *after* the simulation has finished. The **trace** facility is of little practical value, so its use will not be described in this course.

Computer Activity 11.3   Summarizing output

In this activity, you will produce a scatterplot of the simulated values of μ and τ, and kernel density estimates of the marginal posterior p.d.f.s for these parameters, as well as numerical summaries of the values of μ and τ. Only the values from the equilibrium distribution should be used — that is, iteration 101 onwards — so do not change the values of **beg** and **end** that you used in Computer Activity 11.2.

(a) First, create a scatterplot of the simulated values of μ and τ, as follows.

◇   Obtain the **Correlation Tool** dialogue box (**Inference** > **Correlations**).

◇   There are two **nodes** fields in the **Correlation Tool** dialogue box. Type `tau` in the first field, and `mu` in the second field.

◇   Enter 101 in the **beg** field of the **Correlation Tool** dialogue box.

◇   Click on the **scatter** button, and a scatterplot similar to that in Figure 11.2 will be produced.

In Computer Activity 10.3, you produced a scatterplot of sampled values for `mu` and `tau` based on a conjugate analysis of Cavendish's measurements. A scatterplot based on one such sample is given in Figure 10.2. Compare the scatterplots in Figures 10.2 and 11.2. Does the choice of prior appear to affect the relationship between `mu` and `tau`?

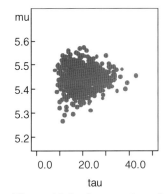

Figure 11.2   Scatterplot of 900 simulated values of μ and τ

(b) Now obtain estimates of the marginal posterior p.d.f.s and numerical summaries of the samples, as follows.

The method is the same as for independent samples.

◇   Type * in the **node** field in the **Sample Monitor Tool** dialogue box (if it is not already there).

◇   In the **Sample Monitor Tool** dialogue box, click on **density**, then on **stats**.

Kernel density estimates of the posterior p.d.f.s for μ and τ are shown in Figure 11.3.

Your kernel density estimates and numerical summaries may be different, but they should be broadly similar to those shown here.

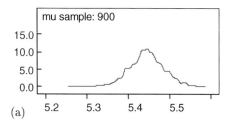
(a)

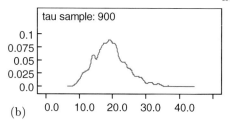
(b)

Figure 11.3   Kernel density estimates of the posterior p.d.f.s: (a) μ (b) τ

The numerical summaries, which are displayed in the **Node statistics** window, are reproduced below.

node	mean	sd	MC error	2.5%	median	97.5%	start	sample
mu	5.444	0.04291	0.001099	5.359	5.444	5.531	101	900
tau	19.52	5.14	0.1976	10.74	19.15	31.36	101	900

Note that for both the kernel density estimates and the numerical summaries, the `sample` size is 900 because the first 100 iterations have been ignored.

Compare the numerical summaries and the estimate of the density for μ with those you obtained in the conjugate Bayesian analysis in Computer Activity 10.3.

Summary of Chapter 11

In this chapter, you have used WinBUGS to obtain samples from a posterior distribution defined in terms of the likelihood and the prior, and to analyse the simulated values. You have learned how to load data into WinBUGS. You have also learned how to produce a trace plot for a subset of the simulated values, and how to analyse the subset.

Chapter 12
Dealing with MCMC samples from multiple chains

In this chapter, you will analyse data on the sizes of 402 'platoons' of vehicles recorded on a section of the Trans-Canada Highway, in Western Canada. The data, which were introduced in Example 10.1 of *Book 4*, are summarized in Table 12.1.

Archilla, R. and Morrall, J. (1996) Traffic characteristics on two-lane highway downgrades. *Transportation Research Part A: Policy and Practice*, **30**, 119–133.

Table 12.1 Platoon size on Ottertail Hill

Platoon size	1	2	3	4	5	6	7	8	9	≥10
Frequency	256	72	33	21	10	4	4	0	2	0

Notice that although there are $n = 402$ observations, these observations correspond to $m = 9$ frequency counts. In Example 18.1 of *Book 4*, the following model for the data was introduced.

If X represents the size of a platoon, then

$$X \sim \text{Borel}(\theta),$$

$$\text{logit}(\theta) = \log\left(\frac{\theta}{1-\theta}\right) \sim N(0, 100^2).$$

This Bayesian model will be used to analyse the data. In the BUGS language, the model can be defined as follows.

```
model
{
    for (i in 1:m){
        zeros[i] <- 0
        phi[i] <- -y[i]*(-theta*i+(i-1)*log(theta*i)-logfact(i))
        zeros[i] ~ dpois(phi[i])
    }
    ltheta ~ dnorm(0,1.0E-4)
    theta <- exp(ltheta)/(1+exp(ltheta))
}
```

The `for` loop defines the likelihood. This has an unusual form because the Borel distribution is not a model that is pre-programmed in WinBUGS. You do not need to concern yourself with the details of the three lines of code within the loop.

See Computer Activity 11.1 for a description of `for` loops.

The third from last line specifies the normal prior for $\text{logit}(\theta)$.

```
ltheta ~ dnorm(0,1.0E-4)
```

The inverse of the logit transformation is

$$\theta = \frac{e^{\text{logit}(\theta)}}{1 + e^{\text{logit}(\theta)}}.$$

You may like to verify that this is the correct inverse transformation.

This is specified in the second from last line.

```
theta <- exp(ltheta)/(1+exp(ltheta))
```

In Computer Activities 12.1 to 12.5, you will use WinBUGS to generate samples of values from the posterior distributions for `theta` and `ltheta` and analyse them. You should try to work through the activities in one session, as they are linked.

WinBUGS will use MCMC to generate samples, so it will be necessary to assess convergence and hence estimate the burn-in period of the simulation. In each simulation so far, WinBUGS has produced a single sequence of sampled values. However, to assess the burn-in period, several sequences of sampled values from the posterior distribution for θ should be obtained, and compared using trace plots, as described in Section 17 of *Book 4*. After deciding on the burn-in period, the remaining simulated values from *all* the sequences will be used to make inferences.

Computer Activity 12.1 Obtaining several sequences of sampled values

In this activity, you will generate three sequences of sampled values, each of 5000 iterations, using MCMC.

First, check the model and load the data, as follows.

◇   Start WinBUGS.

◇   The model definition is in the file **borel-logit.odc**, and the data are in the file **platoon.odc**. Open these files now.

                                                     File > Open...

◇   Obtain the **Specification Tool** dialogue box. (Leave it open for the duration of your session.)

                                                     Model > Specification...

◇   In WinBUGS, check the model in **borel-logit.odc**.

◇   Load the data from **platoon.odc**.

WinBUGS calls a sequence of sampled values a chain. Generate three chains, as follows.

◇   Specify that three chains should be simulated by entering 3 in the **num of chains** field in the **Specification Tool** dialogue box.

◇   Compile the model.

◇   Click on **gen inits** in the **Specification Tool** dialogue box, and initial values for the three chains will be produced. These will be generated from the prior distribution.

All of the quantities in the model that are treated as stochastic nodes in WinBUGS, and whose values are not fixed, should be monitored. In this model, there is one such quantity, namely ltheta. However, the posterior distribution for the traffic intensity θ is also of interest, so theta should also be monitored. Thus the nodes to be monitored are ltheta and theta.

◇   Obtain the **Sample Monitor Tool** dialogue box.

                                                     Inference > Samples...

◇   Specify that the nodes ltheta and theta are to be monitored by entering each in the **node** field of the **Sample Monitor Tool** dialogue box and clicking on **set**. Leave all the other fields unchanged.

◇   Obtain the **Update Tool** dialogue box.

                                                     Model > Update...

Notice that **adapting** is checked. This refers to the fact that the posterior distribution is sufficiently non-standard for WinBUGS to use a special MCMC algorithm to simulate from it. Depending on the particular MCMC algorithm it chooses, WinBUGS will spend either the first 500 iterations or the first 4000 iterations 'adapting' the algorithm to obtain a suitable simulation. The only implication of this that need concern you is that either the first 500 iterations, or the first 4000 iterations, will be unavailable for making inferences.

By watching the **Update Tool** dialogue box as the samples are taken, you will be able to see whether the adaption period is 500 or 4000 iterations.

You may wish to change the entry in the **refresh** field to 1000 to speed up the simulation.

◇   Enter 5000 in the **updates** field of the **Update Tool** dialogue box so that each of the three chains will run for 5000 iterations.

◇   Click on the **update** button to start the simulation.

The tick in the **adapting** box on the **Update Tool** dialogue box will disappear after 4000 iterations. This indicates that the adaption period for the algorithm is 4000 iterations in this case.

Computer Activity 12.2   Assessing convergence

Having obtained three chains of sampled values, the next step is to assess convergence, or at least lack of convergence. The recommended way to assess evidence of lack of convergence is by producing a trace plot of the three chains of values superimposed on the same diagram. Do this now for the samples of values of ltheta and theta that you obtained in Computer Activity 12.1, as follows.

◇   Type an asterisk, *, in the **node** field in the **Sample Monitor Tool** dialogue box.

Notice that in the upper part of the **Sample Monitor Tool** dialogue box, the entries in the two fields to the right of the word **chains** are 1 and 3. This indicates that all three chains will be used in subsequent graphical and numerical summaries obtained using the **Sample Monitor Tool** dialogue box.

By altering these values, single chains, or pairs of chains, could be monitored.

◇   Click on **history**.

Trace plots for ltheta and theta similar to those in Figure 12.1 will be displayed.

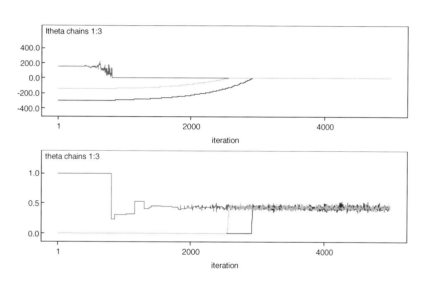

Figure 12.1   Trace plots of three chains of 5000 simulated values of $\mathrm{logit}(\theta)$ and θ

The lines for the three chains begin to overlap shortly after iteration 2500. However, as the initial values for the three chains were very different, the scale of the vertical axes makes it difficult to detect whether the simulated values from the three chains have settled down to the same distribution by iteration 2500.

The point where all three chains begin to overlap may be different in your trace plots.

An important point here is that the chains were simulated using an algorithm which required an adaption period of 4000 iterations. WinBUGS automatically ignores these initial 4000 iterations in its numerical and graphical summaries, so choosing a burn-in value of less than 4000 is pointless.

Verify that 4000 is a sufficient number of iterations to ignore by producing trace plots of the remaining iterations and inspecting them for evidence of lack of convergence, as follows.

◇   In the **Sample Monitor Tool** dialogue box, enter 4001 in the **beg** field. This tells WinBUGS that the first iteration to use in all subsequent numerical and graphical summaries is iteration 4001.

◇   Click on the **history** button in the **Sample Monitor Tool** dialogue box.

Trace plots of the sampled values of `ltheta` and `theta` from iteration 4001 onwards, similar to those in Figure 12.2, will be displayed in another **Time series** window.

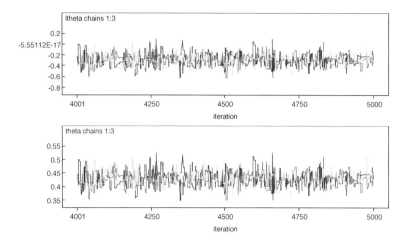

Figure 12.2 Trace plots of three chains of simulated values of logit(θ) and θ, ignoring the first 4000 iterations

The simulated values from iteration 4001 onwards are characteristic of those from the equilibrium distribution of a Markov chain. However, it is hard to see the other two chains under the top chain. So produce trace plots of chain 2 only, as follows.

◇   Enter 2 in both of the **chains** fields in the **Sample Monitor Tool** dialogue box.

◇   Click on the **history** button, and a trace plot for chain 2 will be displayed in a **Time Series** window.

Plots for the other two chains can be obtained by changing the numbers in the **chains** fields. Based on these plots, these values may reasonably be regarded as values from the equilibrium distribution of the Markov chain, and hence as values from the posterior distributions for logit(θ) and θ.

Computer Activity 12.3   *Numerical summaries of simulated values*

Calculate numerical summaries based on the sampled values obtained after the burn-in period of 4000 iterations, including an equal-tailed 95% credible interval for θ, as follows.

◇   If necessary, in the **Sample Monitor Tool** dialogue box, change the values in the **chains** fields back to 1 and 3. Also check that * is in the **node** field, and that the value 4001 is in the **beg** field.

◇   Check that 2.5%, `median` and 97.5% are highlighted in the **percentiles** area.

◇   Click on the **stats** button.

A window entitled **Node statistics**, containing the following entries, will be displayed.

node	mean	sd	MC error	2.5%	median	97.5%	start	sample
ltheta	-0.2949	0.1068	0.004134	-0.49	-0.2935	-0.06518	4001	3000
theta	0.427	0.02611	0.001011	0.3799	0.4271	0.4837	4001	3000

You may not obtain exactly the same numbers as those shown here, but the values you obtain should be broadly similar.

Note that the start iteration is 4001, as the first 4000 iterations have been ignored, and that the summaries are based on 3000 sampled values (three chains of 1000 iterations each).

An estimate of the posterior mean of θ is provided by the mean of the simulated values of `theta`. This is 0.427. The corresponding estimated Monte Carlo standard error (`MC error`) is 0.001 01. The lower and upper limits of the equal-tailed 95% credible interval for θ can be estimated by the 2.5th and 97.5th percentiles, respectively. These give the interval $(0.380, 0.484)$.

One way to assess the accuracy of estimates is by applying the '5% rule of thumb'. This states that the Monte Carlo standard error should be not more than 5% of the sample standard deviation. In this case, 5% of the standard deviation for `ltheta` is 0.005 34, and 5% of the standard deviation for `theta` is approximately 0.001 31. Hence the 5% rule is satisfied for `ltheta` and `theta` (just). Therefore it is reasonable to conclude that the numerical summaries reported are fairly accurate.

Computer Activity 12.4   Running the simulation for longer

By taking a larger sample, more accurate estimates can be obtained. Suppose that you would like to base inferences on a sample of 5000 values for each of three chains. Starting a new simulation from different initial values would require further assessment of convergence. However, this is not necessary if the original simulation is continued from where it finished, since it can be assumed that practical convergence has occurred by iteration 4000. The first 4000 iterations of each chain generated in Computer Activity 12.1 have been ignored as burn-in, so you will need to run the simulation for another 4000 iterations.

Do this now, as follows.

◇   In the **Update Tool** dialogue box, enter 4000 in the **updates** field.

◇   Click on the **update** button in the **Update Tool** dialogue box.

An extra 4000 values for each chain will be generated, starting from where the previous simulation finished — that is, with the simulated values for iteration 5000 as the initial values.

◇   Click on the **stats** button in the **Sample Monitor Tool** dialogue box.

The following numerical summaries based on all the simulated values after the 4000 burn-in iterations will be displayed in a **Node statistics** window.

node	mean	sd	MC error	2.5%	median	97.5%	start	sample
ltheta	-0.2865	0.1026	0.001788	-0.4769	-0.2876	-0.08106	4001	15000
theta	0.4291	0.0251	4.373E-4	0.383	0.4286	0.4797	4001	15000

For both `theta` and `ltheta`, the mean, the standard deviation and the quantiles are similar to those obtained in Computer Activity 12.3. However, the MC errors are less than half as large, indicating that the summaries are more accurate.

Computer Activity 12.5 *Posterior density estimates*

The final, and perhaps most informative, stage in the analysis is to produce
estimates of the posterior p.d.f.s. Obtain estimates of the posterior p.d.f.s of
logit(θ) and θ, as follows.

◇   In the **Sample Monitor Tool** dialogue box, check that * is still in the **node**
field, and that the value 4001 is in the **beg** field.

◇   Click on **density**.

Kernel density estimates similar to those in Figure 12.3 will be displayed.

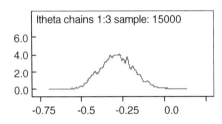 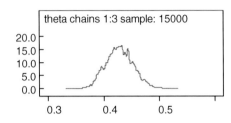

Figure 12.3   Estimates of the posterior p.d.f.s for logit(θ) and θ

The number of values on which the density estimate is based is reported at the
top of each plot. In this case, each is based on 15 000 sampled values — that is,
5000 values from each of three chains.

(a) Use the estimates of the p.d.f.s in Figure 12.3 to describe, in one or two
sentences, the posterior distributions for logit(θ) and θ.

(b) In this model, the prior for logit(θ) was $N(0, 100^2)$. How have beliefs about
logit(θ) changed, after observing the data?

Computer Activity 12.6 will give you some practice at using WinBUGS to
perform MCMC. This combines the procedures described in this chapter.

Computer Activity 12.6 *Lung cancer in Finland*

Data on lung cancer incidence in each of 47 regions surrounding an asbestos mine
in Finland were introduced in Example 18.2 of *Book 4*.

The following Bayesian model for the data was proposed:

$$X \sim \text{Poisson}(\lambda),$$
$$\log \lambda \sim N(\log 5, 0.421^2).$$

Kokki, E. and Penttinen, A.
(2003) Poisson regression with
change-point prior in the
modelling of disease risk around
a point source. *Biometrical
Journal*, **45**, 689–703.

This consists of a Poisson model for X, the number of lung cancer cases in a
region, and a normal model for $\log \lambda$, where λ is the Poisson mean. The prior for
$\log \lambda$ reflects an expert's opinions.

The data are in the file **lungcancer.odc**, and the model is in the file
Poisson-lognormal.odc.

(a) Obtain three chains of sampled values, each of 1000 iterations, using initial
values generated from the prior distribution. Monitor the sampled values of
`lambda` and `llambda`.

Remember that before generating the samples, you must check the model,
load the data, set the number of chains to 3, compile the model, generate
initial values and set the nodes to monitor.

(b) Decide on a suitable burn-in period. Tell WinBUGS to ignore the burn-in values.

(c) Based on the sampled values that remain after burn-in, report estimates of the posterior mean and the equal-tailed 95% credible interval for λ. Use the 5% rule of thumb to decide whether sufficient sampled values have been obtained. If the sample size is not large enough, run the simulation for longer and obtain more accurate numerical summaries.

(d) Produce graphical estimates of the posterior p.d.f.s for λ and $\log \lambda$.

(e) Figure 12.4 shows the prior p.d.f. for $\log \lambda$. Comment on the extent to which the expert's beliefs about $\log \lambda$ have been updated after observing the data.

This model is not complicated enough for WinBUGS to have to 'adapt' its algorithm.

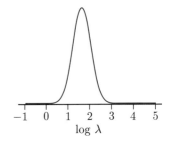

Figure 12.4   Prior p.d.f. for $\log \lambda$

Summary of Chapter 12

In this chapter, you have learned how to obtain several chains of sampled values and use them to assess practical convergence. You have also learned how to use WinBUGS to analyse samples from multiple chains, and how to continue a simulation for further iterations.

Chapter 13
Bayesian random effects meta-analysis

In this chapter, you will use WinBUGS to perform a Bayesian analysis of data from a set of studies which investigated the effect of magnesium on patients with myocardial infarction. The data and their analysis are described in Section 19 of *Book 4*. You should try to work through all the activities in one computer session, as they are linked.

The data come from eight small clinical trials. Patients in each trial were split into two groups: one group received magnesium, while the other group (the control group) was given a placebo. The data are reproduced in Table 13.1.

Higgins, J.P.T. and Spiegelhalter, D.J. (2002) Being sceptical about meta-analyses: a Bayesian perspective on magnesium trials in myocardial infarction. *International Journal of Epidemiology*, **31**, 96–104.

Table 13.1   Data from eight studies into the effect of magnesium on myocardial infarction

Trial number i	Magnesium group Deaths x_i^{M}	Patients n_i^{M}	Control group Deaths x_i^{C}	Patients n_i^{C}
1	1	40	2	36
2	9	135	23	135
3	2	200	7	200
4	1	48	1	46
5	10	150	8	148
6	1	59	9	56
7	1	25	3	23
8	90	1159	118	1157

The Bayesian model that will be used to analyse the data is as follows. For $i = 1, 2, \ldots, 8$,

$$X_i^{\mathrm{M}} \sim B(n_i^{\mathrm{M}}, \theta_i^{\mathrm{M}}),$$
$$X_i^{\mathrm{C}} \sim B(n_i^{\mathrm{C}}, \theta_i^{\mathrm{C}}),$$
$$\theta_i^{\mathrm{C}} \sim U(0, 1),$$
$$\delta_i \sim N(\delta, \sigma^2),$$
$$\delta \sim N(0, 0.0306),$$
$$\sigma \sim U(0, 100).$$

This model is discussed in Subsection 19.3 of *Book 4*.

A distribution for θ_i^{M} is not given explicitly because θ_i^{M} can be calculated from θ_i^{C} and δ_i.

The variables and parameters in this model are defined as follows. For each trial i:

◇ n_i^{M} and n_i^{C} denote the numbers of patients in the magnesium and control groups, respectively;

◇ x_i^{M} and x_i^{C} denote the numbers of deaths in the magnesium and control groups, respectively, which are observations of random variables X_i^{M} and X_i^{C};

◇ θ_i^{M} and θ_i^{C} denote the probability of death for a patient given magnesium and for a patient receiving a placebo, respectively;

◇ δ_i denotes the log odds ratio;

◇   the mean of the normal prior for δ_i is δ, the overall log odds ratio;

◇   the standard deviation of the normal prior for δ_i is σ.

This model makes use of the opinion expressed by several experts that large effects are quite unlikely. This opinion is reflected in the prior for δ, the overall log odds ratio.

In the BUGS language, the model definition is as follows.

You will not be expected to interpret a model definition as complicated as this by yourself.

```
model
{
    for (i in 1:k){
        xm[i] ~ dbin(thetam[i],nm[i])
        xc[i] ~ dbin(thetac[i],nc[i])
        thetac[i] ~ dunif(0,1)
        del[i] ~ dnorm(delta,tau)
        logit(thetam[i]) <- logit(thetac[i])+del[i]
        OR[i] <- exp(del[i])
    }
    delta ~ dnorm(0,prec)
    prec <- 1/0.0306
    sigma ~ dunif(0,100)
    tau <- 1/(sigma*sigma)
    oddsratio <- exp(delta)
}
```

Notice that in this model definition, `xm[1]`, ..., `xm[k]`, `xc[1]`, ..., `xc[k]`, `thetac[1]`, ..., `thetac[k]`, `del[1]`, ..., `del[k]`, `delta` and `sigma` are all treated as stochastic nodes. However, the values of `xm[1]`, ..., `xm[k]` and `xc[1]`, ..., `xc[k]` are known and will be given as part of the data.

In Computer Activities 13.1 to 13.3, you will use WinBUGS to generate samples from the posterior distributions for the parameters and to analyse them. WinBUGS will use MCMC to obtain samples.

Computer Activity 13.1   MCMC simulation

Start WinBUGS. Obtain three chains of sampled values, each of 1500 iterations, as follows.

◇   The model definition is in the file **bayes-meta.odc**. Open the file, and check the model in WinBUGS.

◇   The data, in a format suitable for WinBUGS, are in the file **magnesium.odc**. Open the file and load the data into WinBUGS.

◇   Specify that three chains are to be simulated. (Enter 3 in the **num of chains** field in the **Specification Tool** dialogue box.)

◇   Compile the model.

◇   Generate initial values for the MCMC simulation from the prior distribution.

Specify the nodes to be monitored, as follows.

◇   In the **Sample Monitor Tool** dialogue box, enter the following in the **node** field, clicking on the **set** button after each: `thetac`, `delta`, `oddsratio`, `del`, `OR` and `sigma`.

> Entering `del` in the **node** field and clicking on **set** is a quick way to specify the group of nodes `del[1]`, `del[2]`, ..., `del[8]` to be monitored.

It could be argued that, for the purposes of convergence assessment, it is not necessary to monitor all these nodes. However, if a node is not monitored, and subsequently it is needed for making inferences, then another simulation must be run with the quantity of interest included in the monitored nodes.

◇   Obtain three chains of 1500 iterations.

Notice that for the first 500 iterations, WinBUGS is adapting its algorithm. The simulation should take a few seconds to complete.

Computer Activity 13.2   Convergence assessment

The easiest way to assess the convergence of the three chains to the equilibrium distribution is to inspect trace plots of all the nodes that have been monitored.

There was an initial adaptive phase of 500 iterations, so the burn-in period is at least 500 iterations. Thus it is necessary to inspect traces plots for iteration 501 onwards only. Do this now, as follows.

◇   Enter an asterisk, ∗, in the **node** field in the **Sample Monitor Tool** dialogue box.

◇   Enter 501 in the **beg** field. This tells WinBUGS to ignore the first 500 iterations.

◇   Click on the **history** button.

A **Time series** window will be produced which contains 26 trace plots, one for each of the monitored nodes.

Do the trace plots suggest that a burn-in period of 500 iterations is sufficient?

Computer Activity 13.3 Inference about the odds ratio and log odds ratio

Posterior inferences can be made using the sampled values. The quantity of primary interest is δ, the log odds ratio.

Summarize the samples obtained for the odds ratio, `oddsratio`, and the log odds ratio, `delta`, as follows.

◇ In the **Sample Monitor Tool** dialogue box, check that 501 is in the **beg** field.

◇ Enter `delta` in the **node** field, and click on **stats**, then on **density**.

◇ Enter `oddsratio` in the **node** field, and click on **stats**, then on **density**.

Two **Node statistics** windows and two **Kernel density** windows will be produced.

(a) Use the numerical summaries in the **Node statistics** windows to decide whether or not sufficient samples have been obtained.

(b) Give an estimate of the posterior mean of the odds ratio and an estimate of the 95% equal-tailed credible interval. Does magnesium appear to have a protective effect?

(c) Compare the density estimate for the marginal posterior p.d.f. for the log odds ratio δ with the marginal prior p.d.f. for δ, which is shown in Figure 13.1. How have the experts' beliefs about the overall log odds ratio changed, after observing the results of the eight trials?

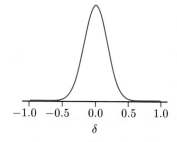

Figure 13.1 Marginal prior p.d.f. for δ

The estimate of the marginal posterior p.d.f. for δ and the numerical summaries of the odds ratio OR suggest the following conclusion from this Bayesian analysis. The evidence that magnesium has a protective effect is very weak, and if magnesium does have a protective effect, then it is very modest. This demonstrates that a Bayesian random-effects meta-analysis with a prior reflecting expert prior opinion would have tempered the early enthusiasm generated by the results of the eight small trials. The random-effects model together with the experts' prior would have provided a more balanced perspective on the results of the eight small trials.

Summary of Chapter 13

In this chapter, you have worked through a case study involving a Bayesian meta-analysis of data from eight clinical trials. You have used WinBUGS to perform a full Bayesian analysis.

Computer Exercises on Book 4

Computer Exercise 1   *Paediatric cardiology*

In Activity 5.9 of *Book 4*, the parameter θ was defined to be the probability that a baby with transposition of the great arteries has heart failure. In Activity 8.2, prior beliefs about θ were represented by the prior Beta$(1.42, 5.13)$. Of 58 babies observed with transposition of the great arteries, five were observed to have heart failure.

(a) Find the prior mode and quartiles of θ.

(b) Calculate the posterior mode and quartiles. How have the beliefs about θ changed after observing the data?

Computer Exercise 2   *Botulism intoxication*

In Example 8.3 of *Book 4*, a gamma/Poisson model was used for μ, the mean number of cases of botulism occurring in a year in England and Wales. The numbers of cases were observed for each of eight years, and the sample mean was 0.75. The prior Gamma$(1.5, 0.5)$ was suggested for μ.

(a) Calculate the 90% HPD credible interval for μ.

(b) Find the posterior probability that μ is less than 1.

Computer Exercise 3   *Nuclear reactor failures*

In Activity 8.3 of *Book 4*, θ was defined to be the failure rate of an HPCI system. The prior for θ is Gamma$(4.7, 4.8)$. The number of reactor failures was observed each year for four years, and the sample mean was 1.75. Calculate the posterior probability that the failure rate is greater than 1.

Computer Exercise 4   *IQ tests*

Some data from an IQ test are described in Exercise 13.1 of *Book 4*. A normal distribution with mean 100 and unknown precision τ was assumed for the scores, and a conjugate gamma prior Gamma$(1 + 1/15^2, 1)$ was adopted. The posterior for the precision τ was calculated to be Gamma$(21.00444, 5220)$.

Interest lies in the posterior distribution for $\sigma = 1/\sqrt{\tau}$, the standard deviation of the scores. If the IQ test is working correctly, then the standard deviation should be 15.

A suitable model definition for use in this exercise is given in the file **IQ.odc**.

(a) Simulate a single chain of $N = 1000$ values from the posterior distribution for σ.

(b) Do you think that WinBUGS used MCMC to do the sampling? Justify your answer.

(c) Produce an estimate of the posterior p.d.f. for σ.

(d) Report estimates of the posterior mean and the equal-tailed 90% credible interval for σ.

(e) Is there any evidence that the IQ test is not working correctly?

Computer Exercise 5   *Mega-trial into magnesium and myocardial infarction*

The data to be analysed in this exercise are from a mega-trial into the protective effect of magnesium on myocardial infarction. The data and model are discussed in Section 19 of *Book 4*.

The model definition is in the file **bayes-megatrial.odc**, and the data are in the file **magnesium-mega.odc**.

(a) Generate three chains of simulated values, each of 5000 iterations.

(b) Do you think that WinBUGS used MCMC to do the sampling? Justify your answer.

(c) Estimate the length of burn-in.

(d) Report an estimate of the posterior mean of the log odds ratio δ. Also report an estimate of the equal-tailed 95% credible interval for δ.

(e) Comment on the accuracy of your inferences.

Learning outcomes

You have been working to acquire the following skills in using *LearnBayes*.

◇ Explore prior to posterior analyses for a proportion.

◇ Explore normal, beta and gamma priors.

◇ Match normal, beta and gamma priors to assessed values of the prior mode and quartiles.

◇ Calculate prior summaries, probabilities and quantiles for normal, beta and gamma priors.

◇ Explore likelihoods for normal, binomial and Poisson data.

◇ Calculate posteriors using normal/normal, beta/binomial and gamma/Poisson models.

◇ Calculate posteriors using uniform/normal, uniform/binomial and uniform/Poisson models.

◇ Produce plots of prior, likelihood and posterior for normal/normal, beta/binomial and gamma/Poisson models.

◇ Produce plots of prior, likelihood and posterior for uniform/normal, uniform/binomial and uniform/Poisson models.

◇ Calculate posterior summaries, probabilities and quantiles for normal, beta and gamma posteriors.

◇ Calculate equal-tailed credible intervals and HPD credible intervals for normal, beta and gamma posteriors.

You have been working to acquire the following skills in using WinBUGS.

◇ Open and close a WinBUGS document.

◇ Print output, and export output for use in other documents.

◇ Interpret a straightforward model definition written in the BUGS language.

◇ Check a model definition.

◇ Load data, given a file containing the data written in an appropriate format.

◇ Compile a model.

◇ Obtain one or more chains of sampled values, given a model definition in a WinBUGS document, with initial values generated by WinBUGS.

◇ Produce trace plots of sampled values.

◇ Use trace plots to assess convergence and choose a suitable burn-in period.

◇ Obtain graphical summaries (kernel density estimates and scatterplots) and numerical summaries of simulated values.

Solutions to Computer Activities

Note that for the solutions involving the use of WinBUGS, you might obtain slightly different numerical and graphical results from those presented here (due to sampling variability). However, your results should be broadly similar.

Solution 2.3

(a) If you place the cross-hairs on the peak of the likelihood, you will see that the value of θ is 0.22 at this point. Since the likelihood is greatest at this point, the most likely value of θ is 0.22.

(b) (i) As the sample size increases, the likelihood gets narrower, although the peak remains in the same place. This means that fewer values are considered likely for θ given the data. The likelihood when the sample size is 250 is shown in Figure S.1(a).

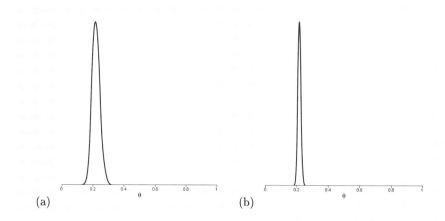

Figure S.1 The likelihood function for θ when the proportion of successes observed is 0.22: (a) 250 trials (b) 2004 trials

(ii) The peak of the likelihood stays in the same place as the sample size increases from 50 to 250, so the most likely value of θ, as suggested by the data, does not change as the sample size increases; it remains 0.22.

(c) The likelihood function is very narrow (see Figure S.1(b)), and is centred around the value $\theta = 0.22$. With a sample size as large as 2004, the data suggest that the value of θ is very close to 0.22.

Solution 2.4

(a) (i)   Figure S.2 shows the likelihood function for $p = 0.5$, $p = 0.9$ and $p = 1$.

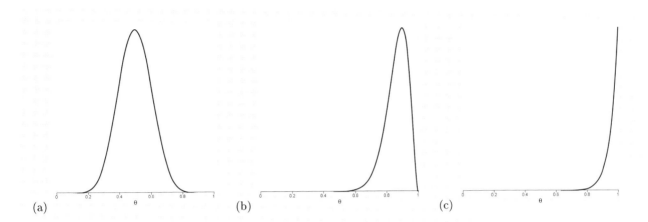

(a)   (b)   (c)

Figure S.2   The likelihood function for θ when the observed proportion of successes in 20 trials is p: (a) $p = 0.5$
(b) $p = 0.9$ (c) $p = 1$

As the observed proportion of successes increases, the position of the
peak of the likelihood moves to the right.

(ii)   The likelihood becomes increasingly asymmetric as the observed
proportion of successes increases.

(b)   As might be expected, the position of the peak of the likelihood moves to the
left as the observed proportion of successes decreases. The likelihood becomes
increasingly asymmetric as the observed proportion of successes becomes
small. Figure S.3 shows the likelihood function for $p = 0.1$ and $p = 0$.

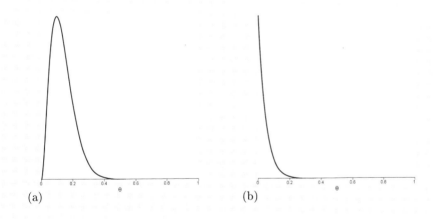

(a)   (b)

Figure S.3   The likelihood function for θ when the observed proportion of
successes in 20 trials is p: (a) $p = 0.1$ (b) $p = 0$

Notice that the likelihood when $p = 0.1$ is the reflection in the line $\theta = 0.5$ of
the likelihood when $p = 0.9$.

(c)   The likelihood has its peak at the point where θ is equal to the observed
proportion of successes. (You can check this by placing the mouse pointer on
the peak of the likelihood.) Thus the most likely value of θ, as suggested by
the data, is the observed proportion of successes.

Solution 2.6

(a) To obtain the plot of the prior, likelihood and posterior, use the method described in Computer Activity 2.5. Enter the values 0.05 for **Lower value**, 0.25 for **Most likely value**, and 0.9 for **Higher value**.

(b) The plot of the flat prior, likelihood and posterior is shown in Figure S.4.

A flat prior represents the fact that there is no prior information about θ, so the likelihood contains all the available information regarding θ. Therefore when using a flat prior, the posterior is the same as the likelihood for observing 6 successes in 9 trials (when the likelihood is scaled so that the area underneath it is 1).

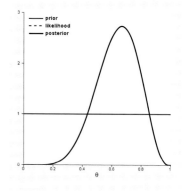

Figure S.4 Flat prior, likelihood and posterior for θ

Solution 2.7

To obtain the plot, use the method described in Computer Activity 2.5. Enter the values 0.15 for **Lower value**, 0.25 for **Most likely value**, and 0.35 for **Higher value**.

The plot of the prior, likelihood and posterior is shown in Figure S.5.

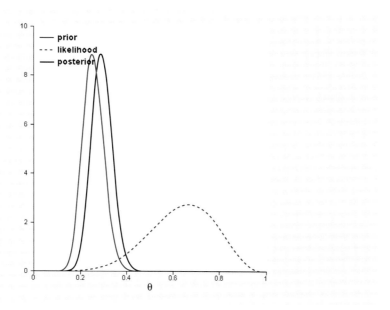

Figure S.5 Prior, likelihood and posterior for θ

In this case, the prior is more informative about θ than the likelihood since the prior is taller and narrower than the likelihood. As a result, the posterior is closer to the prior.

Solution 2.8

(a) As the sample size increases, the likelihood becomes more informative and the posterior moves closer to the likelihood. By the time n is 100, the prior and likelihood are approximately equally informative, so the posterior is approximately midway between them (see Figure S.6(a)).

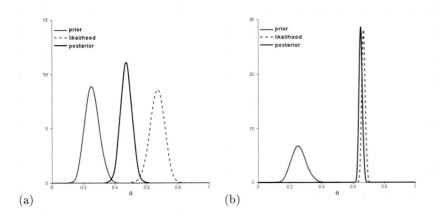

(a)   (b)

Figure S.6 Prior, likelihood and posterior for θ for sample size n: (a) $n = 100$ (b) $n = 2000$

(b) When $n = 2000$, the likelihood is more informative than the prior, and the posterior is closer to the likelihood (see Figure S.6(b)).

Solution 2.9

(a) Prior A, the likelihood after observing 11 'yes' replies from the first 50 interviewees, and the resulting posterior, are shown in Figure S.7(a).

The method is described in Computer Activity 2.5.

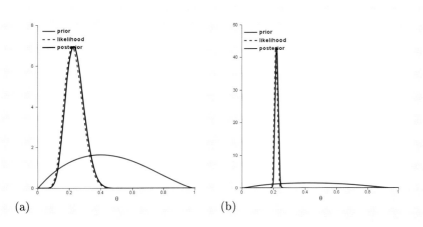

(a)   (b)

Figure S.7 Prior A, likelihood and posterior for θ when the proportion of 'yes' replies is 0.22: (a) $n = 50$ (b) $n = 2004$

Prior A is weak and not very informative in comparison to the likelihood, so it yields a posterior which is close the likelihood. The posterior mean, median and mode are 0.239, 0.235 and 0.229, respectively, indicating that the posterior is slightly right-skew. The posterior standard deviation is 0.057.

The plot of Prior A, the likelihood when $n = 2004$ and the resulting posterior is shown in Figure S.7(b). The posterior mean is 0.221, whereas the posterior median and mode are both 0.22. The posterior standard deviation is 0.009.

(b) After observing 11 'yes' replies from the first 50 interviewees, Prior B is slightly stronger and more informative than the likelihood, so the posterior is closer to the prior than to the likelihood, as shown in Figure S.8(a).

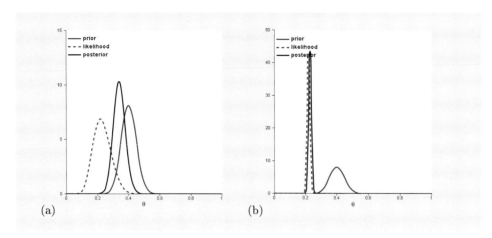

(a)   (b)

Figure S.8 Prior B, likelihood and posterior for θ when the proportion of 'yes' replies is 0.22: (a) $n = 50$ (b) $n = 2004$

The posterior mean, median and mode are 0.341, 0.341 and 0.339, respectively, and the posterior standard deviation is 0.039.

The plot of Prior B, the likelihood when $n = 2004$ and the resulting posterior is shown in Figure S.8(b). In this case, the posterior mean and median are both 0.229, and the posterior mode is 0.228. The posterior standard deviation is 0.009.

(c) When observing 50 interviewees, the posterior beliefs regarding θ are quite different for the two priors: the posterior most likely value of θ using Prior A is 0.229, whereas the most likely value using Prior B is 0.339. In addition, the posterior standard deviation is different for the two priors, representing different levels of uncertainty about θ.

However, after observing all 2004 interviewees, the posteriors using Priors A and B are very similar: the posterior most likely value of θ using Prior A is 0.22, and the most likely value using Prior B is 0.228. Both posteriors have the same standard deviation, so both posteriors represent the same level of uncertainty about θ.

Solution 3.3

(a) The normal prior given in *LearnBayes* is $N(10, 8.792)$.

(b) The normal prior given in *LearnBayes* is $N(10, 219.804)$. The mean remains unchanged. However, the variance has increased greatly as the assessed quartiles are now much further apart.

(c) The normal prior given in *LearnBayes* is $N(10, 879.217)$.

LearnBayes always chooses a normal prior with mode equal to the assessed mode.

To calculate the probability that θ is less than 0, choose P(θ < d) from the drop-down menu in the **Prior probability** area, and set **d** to 0: the probability $P(\theta < 0)$ is 0.368.

To calculate the probability that θ is greater than 40, choose P(θ > c) from the drop-down menu, and set **c** to 40: the probability $P(\theta > 40)$ is 0.156.

The assessed values $L = 0$ and $U = 40$ represent the beliefs that

$$P(\theta < 0) = P(\theta > 40) = 0.25.$$

However, for the calculated normal prior,

$$P(\theta < 0) = 0.368, \quad P(\theta > 40) = 0.156.$$

These are not very close to the required value of 0.25. This suggests that the calculated normal prior may not be adequate to represent the prior beliefs.

Solution 3.5

(a) For Beta(5, 5), the mode is 0.5 and the standard deviation is 0.151. The prior is shown in Figure S.9(a).

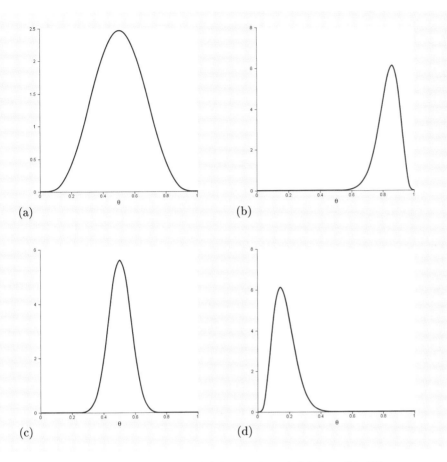

Figure S.9 Beta priors: (a) Beta(5, 5) (b) Beta(25, 5) (c) Beta(25, 25) (d) Beta(5, 25)

(b) As the value of parameter a increases (while b remains fixed), the prior becomes narrower and increasingly left-skew, and the mode increases towards 1 (see Figure S.9(b)).

(c) As parameter b increases, the prior becomes less skewed until b is the same as a. When b is equal to a, the prior is symmetric about $\theta = 0.5$. The mode of Beta(25, 25) is 0.5, and the standard deviation is 0.07. Therefore the mode of this prior is the same as the mode of Beta(5, 5), but the prior is narrower, as reflected by the smaller standard deviation. (See Figures S.9(a) and S.9(c).)

(d) Beta(a, b) is a reflection in the line $\theta = 0.5$ of Beta(b, a), so the prior will become increasingly right-skew and the mode will decrease towards 0. The Beta(5, 25) prior is shown in Figure S.9(d).

(e) Beta(1, 1) is the same as $U(0, 1)$, which is flat for all values of θ between 0 and 1. Thus there is no mode when $a = b = 1$.

Solution 3.6

(a) The parameter values of the beta prior which best matches the assessed prior values are displayed in the **Prior parameters** area. The prior given is Beta(4.6, 11.8).

(b) The mode of the prior Beta(4.6, 11.8) is displayed in the **Prior summaries** area. This is 0.25, the same as the assessed mode.

(c) Using the **Prior quantile** area, the lower quartile of Beta(4.6, 11.8) is 0.201 and the upper quartile is 0.350. These are very close to the assessed quartiles.

(d) The mode and quartiles of the beta prior are very close to the assessed values, so this beta prior is a good representation of the prior beliefs about θ.

Solution 3.7

(a) Using the method described in Computer Activity 3.6, the beta priors are as follows:

$$\text{Set 1: Beta}(2.13, 2.7), \quad \text{Set 2: Beta}(2.27, 2.9).$$

(b) From the **Prior summaries** area, the mode is 0.4 for each beta prior — the same as the assessed mode.

(c) Set **c** to U and **d** to L in the **Prior probability** area. To calculate $P(\theta > U)$, choose P(θ > c) from the drop-down menu, and to calculate $P(\theta < L)$, choose P(θ < d).

For Beta(2.13, 2.7), with $L = 0.3$ and $U = 0.6$,

$$P(\theta < 0.3) = 0.280, \quad P(\theta > 0.6) = 0.240.$$

For Beta(2.27, 2.9), with $L = 0.1$ and $U = 0.45$,

$$P(\theta < 0.1) = 0.031, \quad P(\theta > 0.45) = 0.466.$$

(d) The match between the prior Beta(2.13, 2.7) and the first set of assessed values is quite good: $P(\theta < L)$ and $P(\theta > U)$ are not far from 0.25.

However, the match between the prior Beta(2.27, 2.9) and the second set of assessed values is poor: $P(\theta < L)$ and $P(\theta > U)$ are nowhere near 0.25. In this case, it looks as though a beta distribution should not be used as a prior to represent these beliefs.

Solution 3.8

My mode for θ_{junk} was assessed to be 0.33, and the assessed values of my prior quartiles for θ_{junk} were $L = 0.25$ and $U = 0.55$. *LearnBayes* gives Beta(1.94, 2.9) as the beta prior which is the best match to my assessed values. The mode for this beta prior is 0.33; the lower and upper quartiles are 0.241 and 0.547, respectively. So Beta(1.94, 2.9) seems to provide a good approximation to my prior opinion regarding θ_{junk}. Of course, your beta prior will be different from mine (unless you had exactly the same assessed values!) and it is possible that you may think that your beta prior is *not* an adequate approximation to your prior opinion regarding θ_{junk}.

See the solutions to Activities 6.2 and 6.6 in *Book 4*.

Solution 3.9

(a) The prior mode and mean are given in the **Prior summaries** area; they are 1.25 and 1.50, respectively.

(b) In the **Prior probability** area, enter 2 in the **d** field. This gives $P(\theta < 2) = 0.809$.

(c) Using the **Prior quantile** area, the 0.95-quantile of Gamma(6, 4) is 2.63.

Solution 3.10

(a) The Gamma(2, 2) prior, which is shown in Figure S.10(a), is right-skew. The mode is 0.5 and the standard deviation is 0.71.

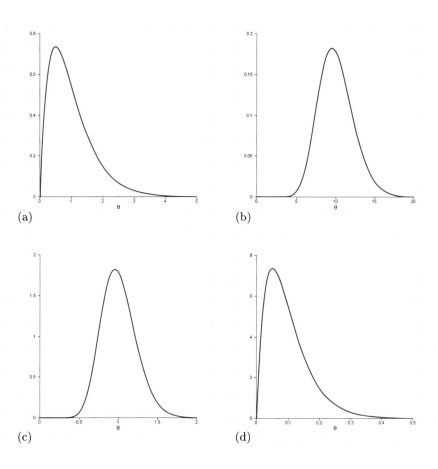

(a)   (b)

(c)   (d)

Figure S.10 Priors: (a) Gamma(2, 2) (b) Gamma(20, 2) (c) Gamma(20, 20) (d) Gamma(2, 20)

(b) As a increases to 20 while b remains at 2, the gamma prior becomes less skewed (see Figure S.10(b)). The location and the spread of the prior also increase: Gamma(20, 2) has mode 9.5 and standard deviation 2.24.

(c) As b increases to 20 (the value of a), the shape of the prior remains the same (see Figure S.10(c)). The mode of Gamma(20, 20) is 0.95, which is one-tenth of the mode of Gamma(20, 2). The standard deviation of Gamma(20, 20) is 0.22, which is also one-tenth of the standard deviation of Gamma(20, 2). Gamma(20, 20) and Gamma(20, 2) have the same shape.

(d) As a decreases (while b remains fixed), the prior becomes increasingly right-skew. The location also decreases — the mode of Gamma(2, 20) is 0.05 and the standard deviation decreases to 0.07. The mode and standard deviation of Gamma(2, 20) are one-tenth of the mode and standard deviation of Gamma(2, 2). The Gamma(2, 20) prior is shown in Figure S.10(d). Gamma(2, 20) and Gamma(2, 2) have the same shape.

(e) Basically, parameter a controls the shape of the gamma prior, while the relative magnitude of a and b controls the location and the spread of the prior.

Solution 3.11

(a) *LearnBayes* suggests the prior Gamma$(4.7, 1.85)$.

(b) The mode of Gamma$(4.7, 1.85)$, which is displayed in the **Prior summaries** area, is 2, the same as the assessed prior mode.

(c) Using the **Prior quantile** area, the lower quartile of Gamma$(4.7, 1.85)$ is 1.68, and the upper quartile is 3.20. These values are close to the assessed values of the lower and upper quartiles.

(d) The mode for the calculated gamma prior matches the assessed mode exactly, and the lower and upper quartiles of the gamma prior are close to the assessed quartiles. Thus it is reasonable to conclude that this gamma prior is a good representation of the prior beliefs about θ.

Solution 3.12

My mode for θ_{phone} was assessed to be 3, and the assessed values of my prior quartiles were $L = 2$ and $U = 5$. *LearnBayes* gives Gamma$(4.4, 1.13)$ as the gamma prior which is the best match to my assessed values. The mode for this gamma prior is 3, and the lower and upper quartiles are 2.54 and 4.94. These values are not too far from the assessed values of the mode and quartiles, so Gamma$(4.4, 1.13)$ seems to provide an adequate approximation to my prior opinion regarding θ_{phone}. Remember that your gamma prior will be different from mine (unless you had exactly the same assessed values), and it is possible that you may think that your gamma prior is *not* an adequate approximation to your prior opinion regarding θ_{phone}.

See the solutions to Activities 6.2 and 6.6 in *Book 4*.

Solution 4.1

(a) The normal likelihood after observing a sample of size 5 with sample mean $\bar{x} = 10$, when $\sigma^2 = 1$, is shown in Figure S.11(a). It is symmetric about $\theta = 10$.

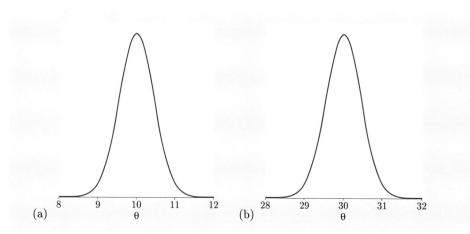

Figure S.11   Normal likelihood when $\sigma^2 = 1$: (a) $\bar{x} = 10$ (b) $\bar{x} = 30$

(b) The shape of the normal likelihood stays the same as the sample mean $\bar{x}$ increases. The only thing that changes is the location: the numbers on the scale on the horizontal axis increase as the sample mean increases. The likelihood when $\bar{x} = 30$ is shown in Figure S.11(b).

(c) The normal likelihood remains symmetric about the sample mean $\bar{x}$, but becomes wider as the (known) population variance increases — look at the scale on the axis as you increase the value of σ^2. The normal likelihood for $n = 5$, $\bar{x} = 30$ and $\sigma^2 = 20$ is shown in Figure S.12(a).

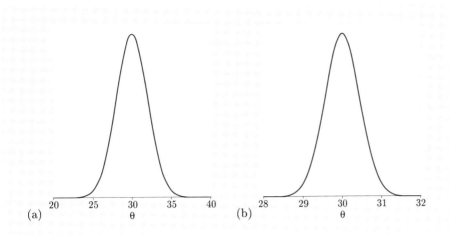

Figure S.12   Normal likelihood when $\bar{x} = 30$ and $\sigma^2 = 20$: (a) $n = 5$ (b) $n = 100$

(d) The normal likelihood remains symmetric about the sample mean $\bar{x}$, but becomes narrower as n increases — again look at the scale on the axis as n increases. The normal likelihood for $n = 100$, $\bar{x} = 30$ and $\sigma^2 = 20$ is shown in Figure S.12(b).

(e) Whatever the values of n and σ^2, the likelihood has its peak when θ is equal to the sample mean $\bar{x}$. Therefore the most likely value of θ, according to the likelihood, is $\bar{x}$.

Solution 4.2

(a) After observing $x = 2$ 'successes' in $n = 10$ trials, the binomial likelihood is right-skew. It is shown in Figure S.13(a).

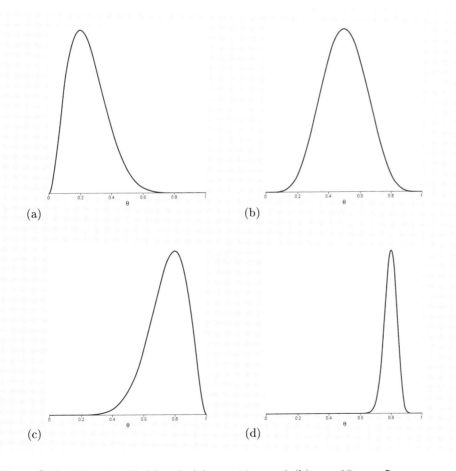

Figure S.13   Binomial likelihood: (a) $n = 10$, $x = 2$ (b) $n = 10$, $x = 5$
(c) $n = 10$, $x = 8$ (d) $n = 100$, $x = 80$

(b) The binomial likelihood is right-skew when $p = 0.2$. It becomes less skewed as p increases towards 0.5, and is symmetric for $p = 0.5$. (The binomial likelihood for $p = 0.5$ and $n = 10$ is shown in Figure S.13(b).) As p increases beyond 0.5, the likelihood becomes increasingly left-skew. (The likelihood for $p = 0.8$ and $n = 10$ is shown in Figure S.13(c).)

(c) The binomial likelihood becomes narrower as the sample size increases. (The likelihood for $p = 0.8$ and $n = 100$ is shown in Figure S.13(d).)

(d) The peak of the binomial likelihood always occurs when θ is $p = x/n$. Therefore the most likely value of θ, according to the likelihood, is p.

Solution 4.3

(a) The Poisson likelihood when $n = 5$ and $\bar{x} = 1$ is shown in Figure S.14(a). It is right-skew.

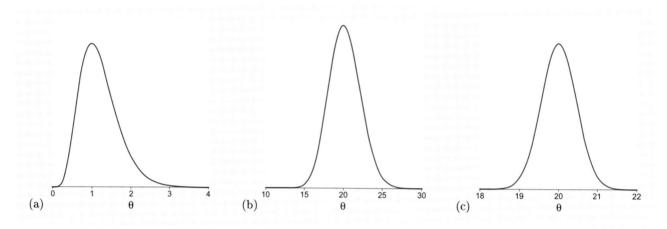

Figure S.14 Poisson likelihood: (a) $n = 5$, $\bar{x} = 1$ (b) $n = 5$, $\bar{x} = 20$ (c) $n = 100$, $\bar{x} = 20$

(b) As $\bar{x}$ increases, the peak of the Poisson likelihood shifts to the right. The likelihood becomes less skewed and, as you can see from the scale on the axis, it increases in width. The likelihood for $n = 5$ and $\bar{x} = 20$ is shown in Figure S.14(b).

(c) As the sample size n increases, the Poisson likelihood gets narrower — look at the scale on the x-axis as n increases. The likelihood for $n = 100$ and $\bar{x} = 20$ is shown in Figure S.14(c).

(d) The peak of the Poisson likelihood always occurs when $\theta = \bar{x}$, so the most likely value for θ, according to the likelihood, is $\bar{x}$.

Solution 5.4

(a) Since $a + b = 8 + 15 = 23$, and this is greater than the sample size n, which is 10, the prior will be more informative about θ than the likelihood. Hence the posterior will be closer to the prior than to the likelihood.

To produce the posterior, set **a** to 8, **b** to 15, **n** (**Number of observations**) to 10, and **x** (**Number of successes**) to 7. (Alternatively, you could set **n** (**Number of observations**) to 10 and **p** (**Proportion of successes**) to 0.7.)

The plot of the prior, likelihood and posterior is shown in Figure S.15.

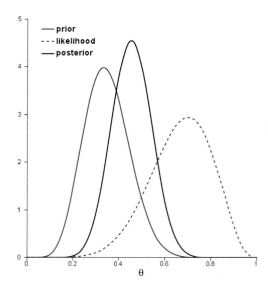

Figure S.15   Prior, likelihood and posterior for θ

As expected, the posterior is closer to the prior than to the likelihood.

(b) As the value in the **m** field increases, the locations of both the prior and the posterior increase. This is to be expected as *LearnBayes* finds the beta prior with mode equal to the value in the **m** field, whose quartiles are closest to the values in the **L** and **U** fields. As the location of the prior increases, the location of the posterior increases. (Notice that for a beta prior, the prior assessed mode need not lie between the assessed quartiles.)

Solution 5.5

(a) The beta prior which best matches these assessed quartiles and mode is Beta$(1,1)$. But Beta$(1,1)$ is simply $U(0,1)$, so these assessed values define a uniform prior. When using a uniform prior, the posterior is equivalent to the (scaled) likelihood. Thus the plot shows the uniform prior, and the posterior and (scaled) likelihood, which are the same.

(b) Changing **m** makes no difference to the prior: it remains Beta$(1,1)$. The reason for this is as follows. The Beta$(1,1)$ prior is a flat prior, so every value of θ is equally likely, and hence every value between 0 and 1 could be considered to be a mode. Therefore whatever value is chosen for the assessed mode, the beta prior which gives the best match when the lower and upper quartiles are assessed to be 0.25 and 0.75, will be the uniform prior $U(0,1)$. Thus changing the value of the mode does not change the beta prior which best matches the assessed values.

Solution 5.6

(a) The mode and quartiles of the prior are found by setting **a** to 1.5 and **b** to 0.5. The prior mode (in the **m** field) is 1, and the lower and upper quartiles (in the **L** and **U** fields) are 1.213 and 4.108, respectively. Notice that, as for the beta prior, the mode for the gamma prior need not lie between the quartiles.

(b) The posterior is found by setting **n** (**Number of observations**) to 8 and **Sample mean** to 0.75. The plot of the prior, likelihood and posterior is shown in Figure S.16(a).

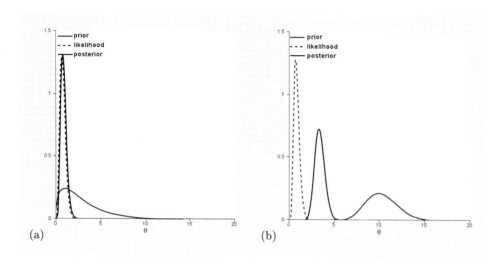

Figure S.16   Prior, likelihood and posterior for θ: (a) mode = 1 (b) mode = 10

Notice that the likelihood and posterior are virtually identical. Thus the data are far more informative than the prior.

(c) The mode of the gamma prior that *LearnBayes* uses is the same as the assessed mode given in the **m** field. Thus, as the assessed prior mode increases to 10, the location of the prior also increases, so the prior and likelihood move further away from each other. When the assessed prior mode is 10, the prior and data conflict with each other. Consequently, as the assessed mode increases towards 10, the posterior moves away from the likelihood to lie between the prior and the likelihood. When the assessed prior mode is 10, the prior, likelihood and posterior are as shown in Figure S.16(b).

Solution 6.1

(a) The following settings are required in the **Normal/normal** option of **Conjugate analyses**.

◇ In the **Prior parameters** area, set **a** to -25 and set **b** to 64.

◇ In the **Assumed known** area, set **Population variance** to 100.

◇ In the **Data summaries** area, set **n** to 20 and **Sample mean** to -36.

The plot of the prior, likelihood and posterior for θ is shown in Figure S.17.

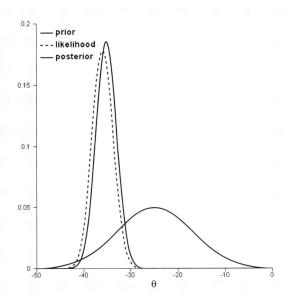

Figure S.17   Prior, likelihood and posterior for θ

In *Book 4*, you saw that the posterior mean is closer to the sample mean than to the prior mean, indicating that the data contribute more than the prior to the posterior. The reason for this is clear from Figure S.17: the likelihood is stronger, and therefore more informative about θ, than the prior.

(b) From the **Posterior summaries** area, the posterior mean is -35.2 and the posterior variance is 4.64. These values are the same as those calculated in *Book 4*.

(c) The probability can be found by choosing P(θ < d) from the drop-down menu in the **Posterior probability** area, with -35 in the d field. The posterior probability $P(\theta < -35|\text{data})$ is 0.538.

(d) The 0.95-quantile of the posterior is -31.66.

(e) A 90% credible interval is obtained by entering 90 in the field in the **Posterior equal-tailed credible interval** area. The interval is $(-38.75, -31.66)$.

For a $100(1 - \alpha)\%$ equal-tailed credible interval (l, u),

$$P(\theta < l|\text{data}) = P(\theta > u|\text{data}) = \tfrac{1}{2}\alpha.$$

Thus l is the $\alpha/2$-quantile and u is the $(1 - \alpha/2)$-quantile of the posterior. Therefore, if $1 - \alpha = 0.90$, then u is the 0.95-quantile of the posterior.

(f) As the posterior is symmetric, the 90% HPD credible interval and the 90% equal-tailed credible interval are the same.

(g) The data suggest that θ is quite a bit lower than was previously believed: the posterior is almost entirely below the value -25, the prior mode.

Solution 6.2

(a) The plot can be obtained as follows.

◇ In the **Prior parameters** area of the **Normal/normal** option, click on the **Uniform** button.

◇ Set **Population variance** to 90, **n (Number of observations)** to 12, and **Sample mean** to 7.5.

The resulting plot of the prior, likelihood and posterior is shown in Figure S.18.

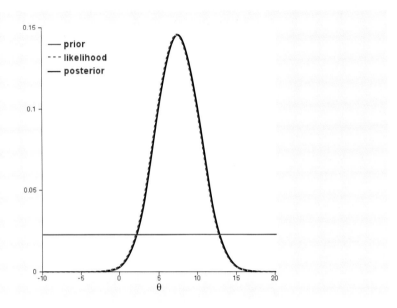

Figure S.18   Uniform prior, likelihood and posterior for θ

As a uniform/normal model is being used, the posterior is a normal distribution. The parameters for this normal posterior are simply the posterior mean and variance. Thus the posterior is $N(7.5, 7.5)$.

(b) The posterior probability that $\theta > 0$ can be found as follows.

◇ In the **Posterior probability** area, set **c** to 0.

◇ Choose P(θ > c) from the drop-down menu.

The posterior probability $P(\theta > 0|\text{data})$ is given as 0.997. Hence, after observing the data, we are almost certain that there is an improvement in scores between the first and second tests.

(c) The 99% HPD credible interval is found by entering **99** in the field in the **Posterior HPD** area; it is $(0.45, 14.55)$. Since the normal posterior is symmetric, the 99% posterior equal-tailed credible interval will be the same.

Solution 6.3

(a) The parameter θ_{junk} is a proportion, so a beta/binomial conjugate model is required. Therefore you need to use the **Beta/binomial** option of **Conjugate analyses**.

My mode for θ_{junk} was assessed to be 0.33, and the assessed values of my prior quartiles were 0.25 and 0.55. I set **L** to 0.25, **m** to 0.33 and **U** to 0.55. The best match to my assessed values is Beta(1.936, 2.9). Remember that your prior is likely to be different.

I received two or more items of junk mail on one day during the week that I collected data, so I set **n** (**Number of observations**) to 6 (the number of days in a week on which mail is delivered) and **x** (**Number of successes**) to 1. The plot of my prior, likelihood and posterior is shown in Figure S.19.

Note that your data are likely to be different from mine, so your likelihood (as well as your prior) will look different from the one shown in Figure S.19.

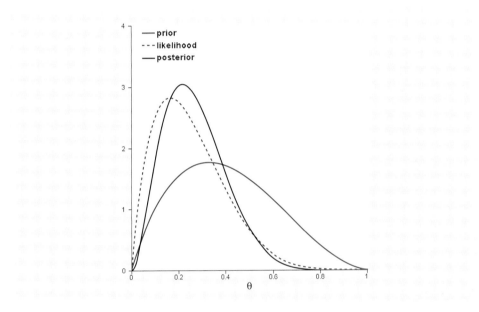

Figure S.19 Prior, likelihood and posterior for θ_{junk}, for my prior and data

My prior is fairly weak in comparison to my likelihood, so my posterior is closer to my likelihood than to my prior. Therefore my likelihood is more informative about θ_{junk} than my prior. You may have defined a stronger prior, in which case your prior will be more informative than your likelihood.

(b) The posterior probability that θ_{junk} is greater than 0.5 is calculated by entering 0.5 in the **c** field and choosing P(θ > c) from the drop-down menu in the **Posterior probability** area. For my posterior, the probability is 0.054. Your posterior probability is, of course, likely to be different.

(c) The 95% equal-tailed and HPD credible intervals are calculated by entering 95 in the fields in the **Posterior equal-tailed credible interval** and **Posterior HPD** areas. The 95% equal-tailed credible interval for my posterior is (0.065, 0.556), and the 95% HPD credible interval is (0.044, 0.522).

The two intervals are unlikely to be exactly the same because the beta posterior is skewed for most posterior parameter values.

Solution 6.4

(a) The parameter θ_{phone} cannot be negative, so a gamma/Poisson conjugate model is required. Therefore you need to use the **Gamma/Poisson** option of **Conjugate analyses**.

My mode for θ_{phone} was assessed to be 3, and the assessed values of my prior quartiles were 2 and 5, so I set **L** to 2, **m** to 3 and **U** to 5. The best match to my assessed values is Gamma$(4.4, 1.133)$. Remember that your prior is likely to be different.

I received 7 phone calls during the week that I collected data, which is more than I expected! I thus have the single observation $x = 7$. Therefore I set **n (Number of observations)** to 1 and **Sample mean** to 7. The plot of my prior, likelihood and posterior is shown in Figure S.20.

Note that your data are likely to be different from mine, so your likelihood (as well as your prior) will look different from the one shown in Figure S.20.

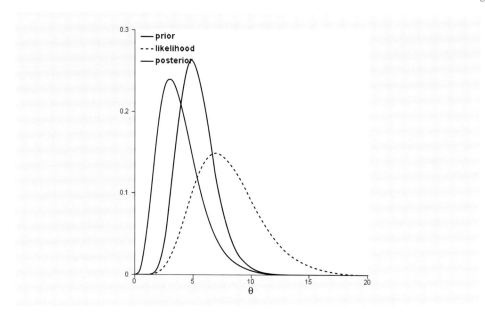

Figure S.20   Prior, likelihood and posterior for θ_{phone}, for my prior and data

My prior is strong in comparison to my likelihood, so my posterior is closer to my prior than to my likelihood. Therefore my prior is more informative about θ_{phone} than my likelihood. You may have specified a weaker prior, in which case your likelihood will be more informative than your prior.

(b) The posterior probability that θ_{phone} is less than 5 is calculated by entering 5 in the **d** field, and choosing P(θ < d) from the drop-down menu in the **Posterior probability** area. For my posterior, the probability is 0.451. Your posterior probability is, of course, likely to be different.

(c) The 95% equal-tailed and HPD credible intervals are calculated by entering 95 in the fields in the **Posterior equal-tailed credible interval** and **Posterior HPD** areas. The 95% equal-tailed credible interval for my posterior is $(2.71, 8.86)$, and the 95% HPD credible interval is $(2.47, 8.50)$.

Solution 8.1

The node Y is followed by the symbol ~, so it is a stochastic node.

In the model definition, both the nodes prec and var are followed by the <- symbol. Therefore they are either deterministic nodes or constant nodes. The node var is a constant node as it is assigned the constant value 8. At first sight, the node prec looks like a deterministic node. However, although it is a function of another node (var), it has a constant value because var is a constant. Thus prec is also a constant node.

Solution 8.2

(a) WinBUGS parametrizes the normal distribution in terms of the mean and precision, not the mean and variance. The precision for this model is 0.5, so the variance is $1/0.5 = 2$, and hence the model is $X \sim N(-5, 2)$.

(b) In this case, $X \sim N(a, 1/b)$, where $a = 6$ and $b = 5$; that is, $X \sim N(6, 1/5)$.

(c) The model is $X \sim B(50, 0.22)$. Remember that WinBUGS puts the probability of success first in the definition of a binomial model.

(d) The model is $\theta \sim \text{Gamma}(2.2, 0.15)$.

(e) The model is $X \sim \text{Poisson}(\theta)$, where $\theta \sim \text{Gamma}(5, 1)$.

Notice that this corresponds to the definition of a full Bayesian model: the data X are modelled using a Poisson distribution with parameter θ, and a conjugate gamma prior for θ is assumed.

Solution 9.3

(a) There is one node, `theta2`, in the file **dogs2.odc**. The code says that `theta2` has a beta distribution with parameters 5 and 15. Hence this model definition corresponds to the model $\theta_2 \sim \text{Beta}(5, 15)$.

(b) Highlight the word `model` in the window entitled **dogs2**. Then obtain the **Specification Tool** dialogue box and click on **check model**. (If you get a message saying `the new model will replace the old one`, then click on **OK**.)

Model > Specification...

(c) Click on **compile** in the **Specification Tool** dialogue box.

(d) Click on **gen inits** in the **Specification Tool** dialogue box.

(e) In the **Sample Monitor Tool** dialogue box, type `theta2` in the **node** field, then click on **set**.

Inference > Samples...

(f) In the **Update Tool** dialogue box, check that the value in the **updates** field is 1000. If it is not, then type `1000` in this field. Click on the **update** button.

Model > Update...

(g) Select `theta2` from the drop-down list of nodes in the **Sample Monitor Tool** dialogue box, then click on the **density** button. An estimate of the posterior p.d.f. similar to that in Figure S.21 will be displayed.

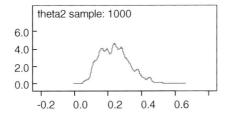

Figure S.21   Kernel density estimate of the posterior p.d.f. for θ_2 based on 1000 sampled values

The estimate of the p.d.f. is highest at about 0.25, so the most likely value of θ_2 is approximately 0.25.

(h) To obtain the required sample quantiles, select `2.5`, `5`, `95` and `97.5` in the **percentiles** area of the **Sample Monitor Tool** dialogue box. The values `2.5`, `5`, `median`, `95` and `97.5` should all be highlighted. Then click on the **stats** button in the **Sample Monitor Tool** dialogue box to obtain the summaries.

Hold down the **Ctrl** key and click on each of these values in turn.

The sample mean (MC error) and standard deviation are 0.243 (0.003 32) and 0.0917, respectively. The 2.5% and 97.5% values can be used to give an estimate of the equal-tailed 95% credible interval for θ_2: $(0.101, 0.449)$. The 5% and 95% values can be used to give an estimate of the equal-tailed 90% credible interval for θ_2: $(0.112, 0.408)$.

(i) The sample mean for θ_2 is 0.243, which is greater than the proportion of samples that you would expect to be identified correctly by chance alone $(1/7 \simeq 0.143)$. However, 0.143 is within the 95% credible interval for θ_2, indicating that the results are consistent with the dogs picking urine samples at random.

Solution 10.2

(a) The node corresponding to the log odds has been given the name `logodds`.

(b) Before obtaining the samples, a few steps must be completed. Use the **Specification Tool** dialogue box to check the model, compile the model and generate initial values. Then use the **Sample Monitor Tool** dialogue box to specify that the node `logodds` is to be monitored.

The samples can be obtained by entering 10000 in the **updates** field of the **Update Tool** dialogue box (and, optionally, 1000 in the **Refresh** field), and clicking on **update**.

(c) Select `logodds` from the **node** drop-down list in the **Sample Monitor Tool** dialogue box. An estimate of the posterior p.d.f. for the log odds can be obtained by clicking on the **density** button in the **Sample Monitor Tool** dialogue box. The density estimate is shown in Figure S.22.

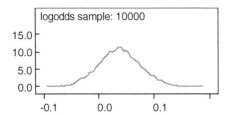

Figure S.22 Kernel density estimate of the posterior p.d.f. for the log odds for a male birth

To obtain the limits for the equal-tailed 95% credible interval, `2.5` and `97.5` must be selected in the **percentiles** area. Clicking on the **stats** button in the **Sample Monitor Tool** dialogue box produces summary statistics. Estimates of the posterior mean (MC error) and standard deviation are 0.038 32 (0.0004) and 0.037 39, respectively, and an estimate of the equal-tailed 95% credible interval for the log odds is $(-0.034\,75, 0.1135)$.

Your summary statistics may be different from these, but they should be broadly similar.

(d) From the density estimate, you can see that $P(\text{log odds} < 0)$ is reasonably small because most of the density lies above 0. However, this probability must be greater than 0.025, because the 2.5th percentile is less than 0.

Solution 10.4

(a) The first two main lines of code in the file are as follows.

```
theta1 ~ dbeta(19,19)
theta2 ~ dbeta(5,15)
```

These are the same as the lines of code in the documents **dogs1.odc** and **dogs2.odc**. They correspond to the models

See Computer Activities 9.1 and 9.3.

$$\theta_1|\text{data} \sim \text{Beta}(19, 19), \quad \theta_2|\text{data} \sim \text{Beta}(5, 15).$$

The third main line of code is as follows.

```
d <- theta1 - theta2
```

This corresponds to the difference between `theta1` and `theta2`, so it defines d correctly as the quantity of interest.

(b) Highlight the word `model` in the document **diffdogs.odc**. Click on **check**, **compile** and **gen inits** in the **Model Specification Tool** dialogue box. Then, in the **Sample Monitor Tool** dialogue box, enter `d` in the **node** field and click on **set**. In the **Update Tool** dialogue box, enter 10000 in the **updates** field (and, optionally, 1000 in the **refresh** field) and click on **update**.

(c) First enter `d` in the **node** field of the **Sample Monitor Tool** dialogue box. Then check that the values `2.5`, `median` and `97.5` are highlighted in the **percentiles** area, and click on **density** and **stats**.

The kernel density estimate of the posterior p.d.f. for d is shown in Figure S.23.

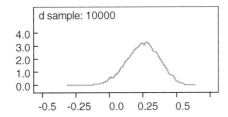

Figure S.23   Kernel density estimate of the posterior p.d.f. for d

An estimate of the posterior mean of d is provided by the sample mean, which is 0.249 (0.001 26). The number in brackets is the Monte Carlo standard error of the mean. An estimate of the equal-tailed 95% credible interval for d is $(-0.003, 0.478)$; this was obtained from the sample 0.025-quantile and the sample 0.975-quantile (rounded to three decimal places).

The equal-tailed 95% credible interval only just includes the value 0, so there is some suggestion that the type of urine used for training makes a difference. However, the evidence is weak.

Solution 11.3

(a) The patterns in the scatterplots in Figures 10.2 and 11.2 are very similar. In both scatterplots, the points form a triangular pattern, with the largest range of values of `tau`, between approximately 10 and 40, being associated with values of `mu` in the range 5.4 to 5.5. Therefore the relationship between `mu` and `tau` does not seem to depend on the choice of prior.

(b) In the conjugate analysis of Computer Activity 10.3, the estimate of the posterior mean of μ was 5.44 (0.001 28) and the equal-tailed 95% credible interval was (5.351, 5.535). In this analysis, the estimate of the posterior mean for μ is 5.44 (0.001 10) and the equal-tailed 95% credible interval is (5.359, 5.531). Thus the results of the two analyses are very similar: the estimates of the posterior mean and the equal-tailed 95% credible interval differ only in the third decimal place. The kernel density estimates of the posterior p.d.f. for μ in Figures 10.3 and 11.3 are very similar.

Solution 12.5

(a) The posterior distribution for $\text{logit}(\theta)$ is roughly symmetrical about -0.3, and the probability that $\text{logit}(\theta)$ takes a value outside the range $(-0.5, 0)$ is low.

The posterior distribution for the traffic intensity θ is roughly symmetrical about a central value of 0.42, and the probability that θ takes a value outside the range $(0.35, 0.5)$ is very low.

(b) The posterior p.d.f. is much more peaked than the prior p.d.f., representing more certainty in a smaller range of values. The information in the prior distribution appears to have been overwhelmed by information from the data.

Solution 12.6

(a) The method is described in Computer Activity 12.1. To simulate the chains for 1000 iterations, make sure that 1000 is entered in the **updates** field in the **Update Tool** dialogue box.

(b) The method is described in Computer Activity 12.2. To assess convergence and choose a suitable burn-in period, trace plots of the three chains of values superimposed on the same diagram are required. Your plots will be similar to those in Figure S.24.

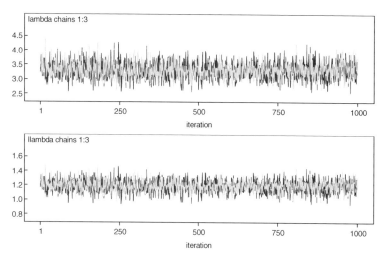

Figure S.24   Trace plots for λ and $\log \lambda$

For each parameter, the three chains overlap for all 1000 iterations, and each chain oscillates randomly around a common mean, with a common variance. This suggests that, to all intents and purposes, equilibrium is reached (almost) immediately. To err on the side of caution, you might decide to ignore the first 100 iterations, though this is not strictly necessary.

This choice of burn-in can be verified by entering 101 in the **beg** field in the **Sample Monitor Tool** dialogue box, and clicking on **history**. Plots similar to those in Figure S.25 will be produced.

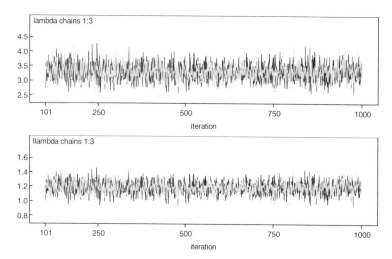

Figure S.25   Trace plots for λ and $\log \lambda$, ignoring the first 100 iterations

(c) The method is described in Computer Activity 12.3. An example of the numerical summaries obtained with a burn-in of 100 is shown below.

node	mean	sd	MC error	2.5%	median	97.5%	start	sample
lambda	3.307	0.2615	0.005028	2.804	3.3	3.839	101	2700
llambda	1.193	0.07913	0.00151	1.031	1.194	1.345	101	2700

The posterior mean of λ is estimated by the mean of the sampled values, which is 3.31 (0.005 03) in this case. An estimate of the equal-tailed 95% credible interval for λ is $(2.80, 3.84)$. For both λ and $\log \lambda$, the Monte Carlo standard error is less than 5% of the corresponding sample standard deviation, indicating that inferences based on these values are probably accurate enough: a larger sample size is not necessary.

(d) The method is described in Computer Activity 12.5. The kernel density estimates of the posterior p.d.f.s for λ and $\log \lambda$ should resemble those in Figure S.26, which were obtained assuming a burn-in of 100.

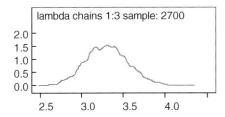 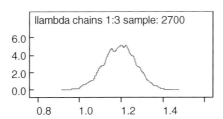

Figure S.26   Estimates of the posterior p.d.f.s for λ and $\log \lambda$

(e) Comparing the estimated posterior p.d.f. for $\log \lambda$ in Figure S.26 with the prior p.d.f. in Figure 12.4, you can see that the data have been very informative about $\log \lambda$. For the posterior distribution, the probability that $\log \lambda$ is less than 1 or greater than 1.4 is very low. The expert's prior assigned considerable probability to a much wider range of values. Also, the expert's prior belief that $\log \lambda$ was about 1.61 has been updated by the data to a posterior belief that $\log \lambda$ is very close to 1.2.

Solution 13.2

In each of the trace plots, the three chains overlap for all 1000 iterations, and each appears to oscillate randomly around a common mean with common variance. This suggests that a burn-in period of 500 iterations is sufficient.

Solution 13.3

(a) The standard deviations of `delta` and `oddsratio` are 0.1709 and 0.1503, respectively. The corresponding MC errors are 0.006 764 and 0.005 788. Thus for each variable, the observed MC error is less than 5% of the standard deviation, and the 5% rule of thumb is satisfied. This suggests that sufficient values have been obtained, so there is no need to run the simulations for longer.

(b) The posterior mean of `oddsratio` is 0.854 (0.005 79), and the 95% credible interval is $(0.616, 1.19)$. This credible interval includes the value 1, so the results are consistent with magnesium not having a protective effect.

(c) The kernel density estimate of the posterior p.d.f. for δ is shown in Figure S.27.

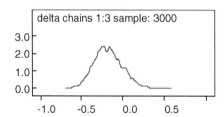

Figure S.27 Kernel density estimate of posterior p.d.f. for δ

The posterior p.d.f. for δ does not differ much from the experts' prior p.d.f. The main difference is that the posterior mean of δ is lower than the prior mean — around -0.25 compared with 0. The variance of the posterior distribution for δ is only marginally smaller than the prior variance. Although the mean of δ has decreased, the value 0, which indicates no protective effect, is still a fairly plausible value.

Solutions to Computer Exercises

Note that for the solutions involving the use of WinBUGS, you might obtain slightly different numerical and graphical results from those presented here (due to sampling variability). However, your results should be broadly similar.

Solution 1

This exercise covers some of the ideas and techniques discussed in Chapters 5 and 6, and in Subsections 8.1 and 9.1 of *Book 4*.

For this exercise, you need to use the **Beta/binomial** option of **Conjugate analyses** in *LearnBayes*. For part (a), you could alternatively use the **Beta** option of **Priors**.

(a) The prior is specified by setting **a** to 1.42 and **b** to 5.13. The prior mode for θ is displayed in the **m** field, and the prior quartiles are displayed in the **L** and **U** fields. Therefore the prior mode is 0.092, and the prior lower and upper quartiles are 0.098 and 0.307, respectively.

Notice that the prior mode is less than the prior lower quartile.

(b) The posterior is found by setting **n** (**Number of observations**) to 58 and **x** (**Number of successes**) to 5.

From the **Posterior summaries** area, the posterior mode is 0.087.

The posterior quartiles are found by first entering 0.25, and then 0.75, in the field in the **Posterior quantile** area. The posterior lower quartile is 0.073, and the posterior upper quartile is 0.122.

After observing the data, the mode has not changed much. However, the posterior is far narrower than the prior, indicating far less uncertainty regarding θ.

Solution 2

This exercise covers some of the ideas and techniques discussed in Chapters 5 and 6, and in Subsections 8.2, 9.1 and 9.2 of *Book 4*.

The **Gamma/Poisson** option of **Conjugate analyses** in *LearnBayes* is required for this exercise.

(a) The prior is specified and the data are entered by setting **a** to 1.5, **b** to 0.5, **n** (**Number of observations**) to 8, and **Sample mean** to 0.75.

The 90% HPD credible interval is found by entering 90 in the field in the **Posterior HPD** area; it is (0.37, 1.38).

(b) The posterior probability $P(\mu < 1|\text{data})$ is found by entering the value 1 in the **d** field, and choosing P(θ < d) from the drop-down menu in the **Posterior probability** area. The probability is 0.681, so it is quite likely that the mean number of cases of botulism per year in England and Wales is less than 1.

Solution 3

This exercise covers some of the ideas and techniques discussed in Chapters 5 and 6, and in Sections 8.2 and 9.1 of *Book 4*.

The **Gamma/Poisson** option of **Conjugate analyses** in *LearnBayes* is required for this exercise.

The prior is specified and the data are entered by setting **a** to 4.7, **b** to 4.8, **n** (**Number of observations**) to 4, and **Sample mean** to 1.75. The required posterior probability is found by entering the value 1 in the **c** field, and choosing P(θ > c) from the drop-down menu in the **Posterior probability** area. The posterior probability $P(\mu > 1|\text{data})$ is 0.797, so it is quite likely that the failure rate is greater than 1.

Solution 4

This exercise covers some of the ideas and techniques discussed in Chapters 7, 8, 9 and 10.

(a) The method is described in Computer Activity 9.1.

(b) The posterior distribution for τ is a gamma distribution, one of the standard distributions that WinBUGS can sample from. Since the standard deviation σ is a transformation of the precision τ, WinBUGS did not need to use MCMC to do the sampling.

(c) Obtaining a kernel density estimate is described in Computer Activity 9.2. A density estimate of the posterior p.d.f. for σ is shown in Figure S.28.

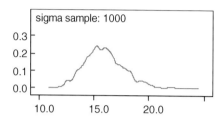

Figure S.28 Kernel density estimate of the posterior p.d.f. for σ

(d) Obtaining numerical summaries is described in Computer Activity 9.2. The following numerical summaries were obtained.

node	mean	sd	MC error	5.0%	95.0%	start	sample
sigma	16.01	1.821	0.04837	13.31	19.32	1	1000

The posterior mean (estimated from this sample) is 16.0 (0.0484). The value in brackets is the Monte Carlo standard error of the mean. An estimate of the equal-tailed 90% credible interval for σ is $(13.3, 19.3)$. (These values are the sample 0.05-quantile and the sample 0.95-quantile of `sigma`.)

(e) From the density estimate of the posterior p.d.f. for σ, a value of 15 is reasonable. Also, 15 lies within the 90% equal-tailed credible interval for σ. Hence these data, combined with the prior information, suggest that a standard deviation of 15 is plausible. There is little evidence that the IQ test is not working correctly.

Solution 5

This exercise covers some of the ideas and techniques discussed in Chapters 7, 11 and 12.

Your answer should be broadly similar to the one presented here.

(a) The method is described in Computer Activity 12.1. After checking the model and loading the data, remember to enter 3 in the **num of chains** field of the **Sample Monitor Tool** dialogue box before compiling the model and generating the initial values. There are two stochastic nodes in the model whose values are not given as data: these are `thetac` and `delta`. Summaries are required only for the log odds ratio `delta`, so specify the two nodes `thetac` and `delta` to be monitored. Finally, enter 5000 in the **updates** field of the **Update Tool** dialogue box, then click on **update**.

(b) Before any samples were generated, the **adapting** box in the **Update Tool** dialogue box was checked. This indicates that WinBUGS used MCMC to generate the samples. This was to be expected since the posterior distribution is given in terms of a likelihood and prior distributions.

(c) The burn-in can be estimated from trace plots of the sampled values. In the trace plots (which are not shown here), the chains overlap after only a few iterations, and the sampled values in each chain appear to oscillate randomly about a common mean with common variance. However, WinBUGS was adapting its algorithm for the first 500 iterations, so the burn-in was at least 500 iterations. A trace plot of the chains from iteration 501 confirms that 500 is a sufficient burn-in.

See Computer Activity 12.2.

(d) An estimate of the posterior mean of the log odds ratio δ is provided by the mean of the remaining sampled values (after ignoring the first 500). The following numerical summaries were obtained.

node	mean	sd	MC error	2.5%	median	97.5%	start	sample
delta	0.05541	0.03092	4.783E-4	-0.004849	0.0556	0.1156	501	13500

For this sample, the estimate is 0.0554 (0.000 478). An estimate of the equal-tailed 95% credible interval for δ is $(-0.0048, 0.1156)$.

(e) The standard deviation of the sampled values of δ is 0.0309. The estimate of the Monte Carlo standard error is 0.000 478, which is less than 5% of the sample standard deviation. It is reasonable to assume that the estimates are fairly accurate.

Index